THEMES AND THESES OF SIX RECENT PAPAL DOCUMENTS

A Commentary

THEMES AND THESES OF SIX RECENT PAPAL DOCUMENTS

A Commentary

by

Most Rev. Robert F. Morneau
Auxiliary Bishop of Green Bay

ALBA · HOUSE   NEW · YORK

SOCIETY OF ST. PAUL, 2187 VICTORY BLVD., STATEN ISLAND, NEW YORK 10314

Library of Congress Cataloging in Publication Data

Morneau, Robert F., 1938-
  Themes and theses of six recent papal documents.

  1. Catholic Church—Doctrines—Papal documents.
2. Catholic Church—Doctrines—History—20th century.
I. Title.
BX1751.M775   1985   230'.2   84-29034
ISBN 0-8189-0482-8

*Designed, printed and bound in the United States of
America by the Fathers and Brothers of the
Society of St. Paul, 2187 Victory Boulevard,
Staten Island, New York 10314, as part of their
communications apostolate.*

1 2 3 4 5 6 7 8 9 (Current Printing: first digit).

Table of Contents

Table of Contents

Preface

The process of internalization, of making something one's own, is an intriguing human experience. On the nutritional level the hamburger easily works its way into our system; more mysterious is the journey of ideas and values into our minds and hearts. One way I have discovered in seeking to grow intellectually is to take the writings of others and enter into dialogue with them by means of a commentary. Personally this has been an enriching and exciting experience.

This volume presents six commentaries on various papal documents written over the past twenty-five years. They have special import in that each of them addresses issues of major human significance. In *Mater et Magistra*, Pope John XXIII addresses aspects of social order in light of Christian principles; in *Evangelii Nuntiandi* Pope Paul VI presents a brilliant vision of the call to evangelization; in *Redemptor Hominis, Dives in Misericordia, Laborem Exercens* and *Familiaris Consortio*, Pope John Paul II deals with a Christian anthropology and the role of Jesus as redeemer, with the experience of God's rich mercy, with the principles of work, and with the values of family life. The intent of each commentary is to whet appetites and get the reader to go to the primary source for a firsthand reading. The articles simply attempt to gather the thoughts of each document into large themes and provide an application to our contemporary situation.

These articles first appeared in *Emmanuel* and *Review for Religious*. I am grateful to Fr. Eugene Laverdiere, SSS, and Fr. Daniel Meehan, SJ, for their gracious assistance in publishing these documents and for the permission to republish them in this single volume.

Copies of the individual Papal Encyclicals in English translation are available from the Daughters of St. Paul, 50 St. Paul Ave., Boston, MA 02130.

Acknowledgments

Grateful acknowledgment is made to the following for permission to use the articles which originally appeared in their publications:

To *Emmanuel*, published by the Congregation of the Blessed Sacrament, 194 East 76th St., New York, NY 10021, for "Effective Evangelization" which appeared in the January/February (Vol. 89, No. 1), March (Vol. 89, No. 2), and April, 1983 (Vol. 89, No. 3) issues of that magazine, and for "Mater et Magistra" which appeared in the May (Vol. 90, No. 4), June (Vol. 90, No. 5), and July/August, 1984 (Vol. 90, No. 6) issues.

To *Review for Religious*, published by the Society of Jesus, 3601 Lindell Blvd., Rm. 428, St. Louis, MO 63108, for the following: "Redemptor Hominis: Themes and Theses," Vol. 39, No. 2, March, 1980; "Dives in Misericordia: Themes and Theses," Vol. 40, No. 5, September/October, 1981; "Laborem Exercens: Themes and Theses," Vol. 41, No. 3, May/June, 1982; and "Familiaris Consortio: Themes and Theses," Vol. 41, No. 4, July/August, 1982.

Acknowledgments

Grateful acknowledgement is made to the following for permission to use the articles which originally appeared in their publications:

Themes and Theses

MATER ET MAGISTRA:
Themes and Theses

Pope John XXIII stirred the imagination of the entire world and touched the hearts of countless people through his warm personality and powerful leadership as head of the Roman Catholic Church. In an excellent biography entitled *Pope John XXIII: An Astute, Pastoral Leader* (Alba House, 1979), Rev. Bernard Bonnot portrays the Holy Father as a man of broad vision and as a skilled administrator and leader. Though the years of his pontificate were turbulent and challenging, John XXIII exercised the fullness of his office with graciousness and expertise.

One of his writings, the encyclical *Mater et Magistra*, provides abundant evidence of faith, vision and professional competence. Four main sections compose this masterly work: (1) a review of the social teaching of Leo XIII's *Rerum Novarum*, Pius XI's *Quadragesimo Anno*, and Pius XII's radio talk in 1941; (2) a further explanation and development of *Rerum Novarum*, considered to be the *magna carta* in our Catholic understanding of the economic and social order; (3) new aspects of the social questions as seen in the early 1960's; (4) the need for the reconstruction of our social relationships in truth, justice and love. This document is rich in content, challenging in its ideals and confrontative of the existential social order. Its publication in May, 1961, demanded considerable courage. Fulfilling his prophetic mission, Pope John XXIII boldly proclaimed the role the Church must play in the life of society, the role of the Church in the modern world.

This chapter attempts to focus on several major themes which are interwoven throughout the encyclical. By concentrating on these specific topics we can deepen our understanding of the Church's social teaching. Each theme is given a broader context in a thesis and this general statement is followed by supporting quotations and a commentary.

It is over twenty years since the publication of the encyclical. The problems it addresses still remain to disfigure our fragile world. Perhaps by listening again to the challenge, perhaps by re-reading the visions of a Pope so committed to God and the human family, perhaps by internalizing the ideals of justice, truth and love will we bring that peace, which is no longer "piecemeal peace," to our humble planet.

THEME 1: HUMAN DIGNITY

THESIS: *The worth and greatness of every person is rooted in his or her relationship with God; thus, every facet of life must respect that intrinsic dignity.*

> Wherefore, whatever the progress in technology and economic life, there can be neither justice nor peace in the world, so long as men fail to realize how great is their dignity; for they have been created by God and are His children. We speak of God, who must be regarded as the first and final cause of all things He has created. Separated from God, man becomes monstrous to himself and others. Consequently, mutual relationships between men absolutely require a right ordering of the human conscience in relation to God, the source of all truth, justice and love. (215)

> For a citizen has a sense of his own dignity when he contributes the major share to progress in his own affairs. (151)

> Consequently, if the organization and structure of economic life be such that the human dignity of workers is compromised, or their sense of responsibility is weakened, or their freedom of action is removed, then we judge such an economic order to be unjust, even though it produces a vast amount of goods, whose distribution conforms to the norms of justice and equity. (83)

"Progress is our most important product!" Thus reads a well-known slogan. Catholic social teaching has a different motto: "Human dignity is the cornerstone of meaning and happiness." An affluent society is characterized by air-conditioned unhappiness—that situation in which people have the finest of everything but inwardly lack a sense of worth and significance. Throughout history the temptation has been the same: choosing things over relationships. Human dignity is a relational experience. It happens when an individual or a community comes to have a felt-sense that through love and mutual concern one is properly ordered in relating to God and others. Both the vertical relationship with God and the horizontal relationship with other pilgrims must be protected and integrated for dignity to be a lived experience. Without God there is no ultimate concern. Without human companionship we live in hellish isolation. Peace comes when both dimensions of life are nurtured and sustained.

Anwar el-Sadat, in his autobiography *In Search of Identity*, speaks of the source of dignity and the resulting peace:

> Ideally the relationship between man and God should be based not on fear (or punishment and reward) but on a

much loftier value, the highest—friendship. The Creator is merciful, just and loving; He is all powerful because He created everything. If you have Him for a friend, and establish a bond of mutual love between you, you will always have peace of mind whatever the circumstances.[1]

Friendship is a major source of dignity and peace. But the encyclical goes further. Cut off from God, the human person becomes monstrous. In our own century we have seen the horror that happens when individuals and societies separate themselves from God's love and his divine imperatives: millions of people destroyed in gas chambers; bombs indiscriminately dropped on thousands of innocent and defenseless people; races excluded from sharing in life because of ethnic traits and skin color. Dignity stripped from the soul! All sense of worth smashed by godless and faithless activity! Without God dignity loses its foundation.

Freedom and responsibility undergird human dignity. These powers and gifts are graces of God meant to be exercised and developed. Yet systems and vested interests threaten their expression and growth. Like a mouse before a cat, individuals become the plaything of unscrupulous corporations and institutions. Personal dignity vanishes when people cannot plan their future or assume responsibility for their choices. Many elderly die not from old age but from dignity denied; many employees, the object of manipulation and exploitation, become listless of heart and weary in spirit; artists, unappreciated and underpaid, despair and shelve their gifts. Simone Weil, in her compassionate understanding of the worker, writes: "Those who people the factory do not feel them [simple joys], except in rare and fleeting moments, for they are not free."[2] No freedom, no dignity! No dignity, no joy! Without joy human existence becomes unbearable.

THEME 2: GOD

THESIS: *God is the source of human dignity; without God, the ultimate foundation of justice and peace, the greatness of the human person loses ultimate significance.*

However, the guiding principles of morality and virtue can be based only on God; apart from Him, they necessarily collapse. For man is composed not merely of body, but of soul as well, and is endowed with reason and freedom. Now such a composite being absolutely requires a moral law rooted in religion, which, far better than any external force or advantage, can contribute to the resolution of problems affecting the lives of individual citizens or groups of citizens, or with a bearing upon single States or all States together. (208)

Indeed, all must regard the life of man as sacred, since from its inception, it requires the action of God the Creator. Those who depart from this plan of God not only offend His divine majesty and dishonor themselves and the human race, but they also weaken the inner fibre of the commonwealth. (194)

However, no folly seems more characteristic of our time than the desire to establish a firm and meaningful temporal order, but without God, its necessary foundation. Likewise, some wish to proclaim the greatness of man, but with the source dried up from which such greatness flows and receives nourishment: that is, by impeding and, if it were possible, stopping the yearning of souls for God. (217)

Mountain climbers do not engage in their risky adventures without being able to return to a camp that provides food, supplies and shelter. Only a fool would venture into the mountain peaks without such a home base. Yet, as individuals and as nations, the attempt to travel the heights of risky social living is done without God who is the source of human dignity, the guide of our moral lives, the one who sustains human effort with grace. History records the events of godless climbs: war, injustice, anomie, despair, fear. History also documents those glorious moments when faith was lived and love was experienced. Here we find charity, hospitality, trust, justice and peace. The kingdom breaking through the darkness because God was taken seriously.

The social teaching of the Church focuses on the heart of the matter. Apart from God the human person collapses, the moral law turns to legalism, the temporal order loses its foundation. Biblical imagery is eloquent in its simplicity: the branch apart from the vine withers. Social systems and relationships cut off from their roots receive the same fate. Social life can be sustained by external forces for just so long. Eventually without the inner dynamism of grace and truth, the structure crumbles. Generations keep trodding the same path hoping to build a strong society and yet lacking proper foundations. The common Fatherhood of God, the spiritual solidarity which bonds all people, is simply not acknowledged. Without this unifying Love, alienation becomes a way of life and apathy, an expectation.

When God is rejected or ignored by society an atmosphere is established that impedes the common person from belief. In Bernard Malamud's *The Fixer* we witness the disbelief of a common man because of what people do to him: torture, imprisonment, hatred, lying, discrimination. The fixer, who can mend everything but the human heart, reflects:

> 'In the beginning was the word,' but it wasn't his. That's the way I look at it now. Nature invented itself and also man. Whatever was there was there to begin with. Spinoza said so. It sounds fantastic but it must be true. When it comes down to basic facts, either God is our invention and can't do anything about it, or he's a force in Nature but not in history. A force is not a father. He's a cold wind and try and keep warm. To tell the truth, I've written him off as a dead loss.[3]

What if the societal, religious and political systems had provided the fixer with opportunity, freedom and some dignity? What if social relationships had been instruments of grace and hope? Belief in God is radically conditioned by the cultural air we breathe.

THEME 3: RESPONSIBILITY

THESIS: *Responsibility must be exercised if people are to grow and maintain dignity.*

But as these various forms of association are multiplied and daily extended, it also happens that in many areas of activity, rules and laws controlling and determining relationships of citizens are multiplied. As a consequence, opportunity for free action by individuals is restricted within narrower limits. Methods are often used, procedures are adopted, and such an atmosphere develops wherein it becomes difficult for one to make decisions independently of outside influences, to do anything on his own initiative, to carry out in a fitting way his rights and duties, and to fully develop and perfect his personality. Will men perhaps then become automatons, and cease to be personally responsible as these social relationships multiply more and more? (62)

Finally, attention is drawn to the fact that the greater amount of responsibility desired today by workers in productive enterprises, not merely accords with the nature of man, but also is in conformity with historical developments in the economic, social, and political fields. (93)

Finally, we cannot pass over in silence the fact that economic enterprises undertaken by the State or by public corporations should be entrusted to citizens outstanding in skill and integrity, who will carry out their responsibilities to the commonwealth with a deep sense of devotion. Moreover, the activity of these men should be subjected to careful and continuing supervision, lest, in the administration of the State itself, there develop an

> economic imperialism in the hands of a few. For such a
> development is in conflict with the highest good of the
> commonwealth. (118)

There are several images and symbols that speak powerfully to the twentieth century person: the picture of the
earth taken from the moon; the mushroom cloud over
Hiroshima telling of tragic death; the crematoriums of
World War II. There is yet another symbol which, when
carefully analyzed, causes fear and trepidation in the human
heart. That symbol is the robot. A robot conforms to every
external command of its master, is unable to be self-
initiating, has no relationship of a personal and affective
nature, is used and manipulated primarily for production.
Its voice is without inflection, its eyes vacant, its actions
stilted and uncaring. No responsibility is assumed nor expected. The encyclical warns of people becoming automatons, a warning that we have not taken seriously enough.

Symbols are of great importance:

> Symbols transform the horizons of man's life, integrate his
> perception of reality, alter his scale of values, reorient his
> loyalties, attachments, and aspirations in a manner far ex-
> ceeding the powers of abstract conceptual thought.[4]

We are in need of finding symbols and images that
depict us as free and responsible. A popular singer will cry
out "Born Free"; contemporary movies unfold the struggle
with responsibility (*My Dinner with Andre*, *Chariots of Fire*);
novels trace the search for responsible living (Potok's *My
Name is Asher Lev*, Gordon's *Final Payments*). On all sides our
freedom and responsibility are threatened by inner and
outer forces. We need to resist yielding to worlds that attempt to control and manipulate. While admitting limitations and finiteness, we still must make personal decisions.
Perhaps the universal image of crossroads continues to vis-

ualize the challenge to accept and assume responsibility. Despite road blocks and detours, our personal and communal journey provides multiple choices and serious responsibility.

Thomas Hardy, that skilled craftsman of word and character, presents an atmosphere that is devastating to mature responsible living:

> Yet, instead of blaming herself for the issue she laid the fault upon the shoulders of some indistinct, colossal Prince of the World, who had framed her situation and ruled her lot.[5]

These reflections of a previous century aptly apply to our own. The colossal prince today goes by the title of "technological society." It controls our values, it controls our time, it controls our life style. Supposedly helpless in the systems and complex structures of our times, individuals abdicate. *1984* has come, figuratively and literally. Our response must be to reject this moral excuse of a colossal prince and begin to assume a committed love and responsibility for our fragile planet.

THEME 4: COMMON GOOD

THESIS: *The ideal of the common good must be understood, protected and promoted with urgent concern.*

> . . . it is necessary that public authorities have a correct understanding of the common good. This embraces the sum total of those conditions of social living, whereby men are enabled more fully and more readily to achieve their own perfection. (65)

> Considering the common good on the national level, the following points are relevant and should not be overlooked: to provide employment for as many workers as possible; to take care lest privileged groups arise even among the workers themselves; to maintain a balance between wages and prices; to make accessible the goods

and services for a better life to as many persons as possible; either to eliminate or to keep within bounds the inequalities that exist between different sectors of the economy—that is, between agriculture, industry and services; to balance properly any increases in output with advances in services provided to citizens, especially by public authority; to adjust, as far as possible, the means of production to the progress of science and technology; finally, to ensure that the advantages of a more humane way of existence not merely subserve the present generation but have regard for future generations as well. (79)

It seems characteristic of our times to vest more and more ownership of goods in the State and in other public bodies. This is partially explained by the fact that the common good requires public authorities to exercise ever greater responsibilities. However, in this matter, the principle of subsidiarity, already mentioned, is to be strictly observed. For it is lawful for States and public corporations to expand their domain of ownership only when manifest and genuine requirements of the common good so require, and then with safeguards, lest the possession of private citizens be diminished beyond measure, or, what is worse, destroyed. (117)

Emerson once reflected: "Beware of too much good staying in your hand." The advice or warning is relevant to our day. Rampant individualism precludes a sense of genuine community. Such a posture makes the realization of the common good impossible. The common good is that situation and atmosphere in which there are sufficient material goods, psychological supports and spiritual opportunities to allow for a fully human life. When too much good stays in the hands and hearts of individual persons or individual nations, the common good is denied existence. With such a denial, human persons lose hope.

The common good is an abstract concept making comprehension difficult. However, its reality is quite concrete and cannot be accused of "weak specification": employment opportunities, accessible goods and services, equality in the economic-political arena, shared responsibility and power. These concrete matters are the substance of a life style that promotes authentic human living. They are provided when authority at every level (government, churches, homes, institutions) realizes that its very existence is premised on its call to realize the common good. The common good doesn't just happen. It demands planning and sacrifice, good will and dedication, expertise and integrity.

The evidence of history, both secular and religious, narrates frequent failure regarding the promotion and protection of the common good. The reasons for this are numerous: extensive personal and communal sin—"For the sin from which Jesus has redeemed us extends over the whole of mankind, including his economic, social and political relationships, and not simply the inwardness of his heart";[6] pervasive and devastating indifference—"Everybody gets so indifferent that I was surprised to know you thought of me";[7] paralyzing fear—". . . to be gripped by fear is, I believe, the most degrading of all emotions for a human being. In fear personality disintegrates, the human will is paralyzed, and man acts as an automaton."[8] Sin, apathy, fear—impediments to the grace, commitment and trust that foster the common good of all. Under the superficial niceties of life there is a violent struggle between good and evil, between our commonness and individualism, between caring and narcissism. The torch of the common good must be held high as an ideal toward which we all strive.

THEME 5: INDIVIDUAL GOOD

THESIS: *Every person has the right to individual goods that protect and promote human dignity; every person also has the right to secure these goods in freedom.*

For the right of private property, including that pertaining to goods devoted to productive enterprises, is permanently valid. Indeed, it is rooted in the very nature of things, whereby we learn that individual men are prior to civil society, and hence, that civil society is to be directed toward man as its end. Indeed, the right of private individuals to act freely in economic affairs is recognized in vain, unless they are at the same time given an opportunity of freely selecting and using things necessary for the exercise of this right. Moreover, experience and history testify that where political regimes do not allow to private individuals the possession also of productive goods, the exercise of human liberty is violated or completely destroyed in matters of primary importance. Thus it becomes clear that in the right of property, the exercise of liberty finds both a safeguard and a stimulus. (109)

As relationships multiply between men, binding them more closely together, commonwealths will more readily and appropriately order their affairs to the extent these two facts are kept in balance: (1) the freedom of individual citizens and groups of citizens to act autonomously, while cooperating one with the other; (2) the activity of the State whereby the undertakings of private individuals and groups are suitably regulated and fostered. (66)

Our predecessors have always taught that in the right of private property there is rooted a social responsibility. Indeed, in the wisdom of God the Creator, the overall supply of goods is assigned, first of all, that all men lead a decent life. (119)

The individual and social nature of the human person creates a healthy tension. Our feet straddle two worlds (actually many more) and the demands of each are legitimate. Difficulty arises when the tension is abandoned and only one side of human nature is acknowledged. Emphasis on individuality can easily slip over into that rugged individualism that excludes any thought for the larger world community and its many needs. Emphasis on the social dimension of life may well lead to the exclusion of personal uniqueness with the resultant form of socialism that destroys an individual's freedom. The pendulum has swung often to the far right and then to the far left. With the weights of truth and insight the pendulum can be confined to balanced parameters.

The present encyclical brilliantly acclaims the common good while at the same time demanding that individual freedom and possession of personal property be safeguarded. The basic principle which has always been operative in the teaching of the Church is that the individual is prior to society. Totalitarianism is an ideology radically opposed to a Christian anthropology. The Christian theory of the human person is grounded on creatureliness and creativity. To offset the danger of getting caught in navel-gazing personal sanctification, our Christian vision flows also out of an ecclesiology: we belong to a community of believers and find our identity and destiny in this context. Our uniqueness is balanced by our universality; the I is seen in relation to the We; the rights of the individual and the rights of the larger society are to be safeguarded, be that community the church, a nation, a home.

The need to protect freedom while retaining a sense of social responsibility has been the subject of reflection by many writers:

> Mental and emotional liberty are not so simple as they look. Really they require almost as careful a balance of laws and conditions as do social and political liberty.[9]
>
> Freedom and life are earned by those alone
> Who conquer them each day anew.[10]

But in the midst of the freedom he had attained Harry suddenly became aware that his freedom was a death and that he stood alone. The world in an uncanny fashion left him in peace. Other men concerned him no longer. He was not even concerned about himself.[11]

The exercise of freedom allows us to maintain a degree of dignity and to possess what is necessary for our well-being. A sense of responsibility and a call to cooperation contextualizes our freedom in a realistic perspective. The balance is difficult and crucial.

THEME 6: JUSTICE

THESIS: *Although justice is a primary goal of Christian teaching, it faces many difficulties in its implementation.*

Although the word *justice* and the related term *demands of justice* are on everyone's lips, such verbalizations do not have the same meaning for all. Indeed, the opposite frequently is the case. Hence, when leaders invoke justice or the demands of justice, not only do they disagree as to the meaning of the words, but frequently find in them an occasion of serious contention. And so they conclude that there is no way of achieving their rights or advantages, unless they resort to force, the root of very serious evils. (206)

It is indeed difficult to apply teaching of any sort to concrete situations, it is even more so when one tries to put into practice the teaching of the Catholic Church regarding social affairs. This is especially true for the following reasons: there is deeply rooted in each man an instinctive and immoderate love of his own interests; today there is widely diffused in society a materialistic philosophy of life; it is difficult at times to discern the demands of justice in a given situation. (229)

But social norms of whatever kind are not only to be explained but also applied. This is especially true of the Church's teaching on social matters, which has truth as its guide, justice as its end, and love as its driving force. (226)

The scale of justice is a fitting image depicting the delicacy of maintaining a balance in the social order. One side of the scales is laden with duties and obligations that people are to conscientiously fulfill; the scale is balanced on the other side by a charter of rights that need to be protected and promoted if human dignity is to be sustained. Various forces can easily throw the scale out of balance: vested interests, dehumanizing ideologies, rampant apathy. As the pages of history are examined, one wonders with amazement that the process of seeking justice has not been forsaken. Hope does spring eternal!

Justice, that moral virtue securing human rights and demanding the exercise of one's obligations, does not stand alone. On either side are its necessary companions: truth and love. Emerson knew well that "truth is the summit of being; justice is the application of it to affairs."[12] Justice, being somewhat blindfolded, needs a guide and a light. Through the use of reason (and for Christians the gift of faith) a certain perception of the meaning of life is gained. Without that vision, justice has no standard and fails to act. Ancient and medieval philosophers were correct in stating that prudence (that perfected ability to make right decisions) is the mother/queen of all virtue. Justice is sired by truth.

The other flank of justice is love, "its driving force." Romano Guardini understood well the linkage between justice and love:

> Man is really just only when he seeks more than mere justice. More not merely quantitatively, but qualitatively. He must find a power capable of breaking the ban of injustice, something strong enough and big enough to intercept aggression and disarm it: love.[13]

The demands of justice are so strong at times that implementation tends to disregard careful consideration of means. In fact, an innate tendency to use force comes into play, a force that easily encroaches upon the rights of others. The result is often an increase of injustice rather than a securing of peace. Another force is called for, i.e., the force of love. This love must be strong and gentle, realistic and deep. Without love the confrontation with injustice will be devoid of mercy—and without mercy, there will never be peace.

The tension between the ideal and the real world is a universal experience. Aldo Leopold, in spite of his love for nature and his desire for ecological wholeness, was a realist:

> We shall never achieve harmony with land, any more than we shall achieve absolute justice or liberty for people. In these higher aspirations the important thing is not to achieve, but to strive. It is only in mechanical enterprises that we can expect that early or complete fruition of effort which we call "success."[14]

The circumstances in which justice is sought are complex. While not despairing in our attempt to comprehend the nature of disputes or the various claims of justice, we must realize that we seek the ideal surrounded by ambiguity and no small ambivalence. Though our expectations are limited, our enthusiasm must not be. We strive with all our energy to incarnate that moral virtue which, when realized to whatever degree, is accompanied by that precious gift of peace.

THEME 7: CHURCH
THESIS: *The Church embraces every human concern and seeks to be solicitous of the whole person.*

Hence, although Holy Church has the special task of

sanctifying and of making them sharers of heavenly blessings, she is also solicitous for the requirements of men in their daily lives, not merely those relating to food and sustenance, but also to their comfort and advancement in various kinds of goods and in varying circumstances of time. (3)

The role of the Church in our day is very difficult: to reconcile this modern respect for progress with the norms of humanity and of the Gospel teaching. Yet, the times call the Church to this role; indeed, we may say, earnestly beseech her, not merely to pursue the higher goals, but also to safeguard her accomplishments without harm to herself. (256)

For it is a question here of the teaching of the Catholic and Apostolic Church, mother and teacher of all nations, whose light illumines, sets on fire, inflames. Her warning voice, filled with heavenly wisdom, reaches out to every age. Her power always provides efficacious and appropriate remedies for the growing needs of men, for the cares and solicitudes of this mortal life. (262)

An understanding of the nature and mission of the Church demands constant study, prayer and clarification. The question of identity and purpose are always with us. One response is to opt for a transcendent model in which the Church removes herself from political, social and economic affairs. The "spiritual" task is central and the focus is on the kingdom beyond, not on *this* world. Historical pains, evils within our systems, complexities of various ideologies are simply too temporal to consume the time and energy of religion which focuses on ultimate concerns and eternity. The present encyclical rejects such a position. Rather the Church must identify herself with the very mission of Christ which reached out to the needy, brought freedom to the downtrodden and despairing, and reconciled all creation to the Father. The documents of Vatican II make it clear that we are a Church *in* the modern world, not the Church *and* the modern world.

A rigid institutional model can no longer sustain the demands of this encyclical. The goals of the Church are far ranging, the variety of ministries too abundant, the changing circumstances of the times too complex for just a few individuals to attempt to fulfill the mission of Jesus. All the people of God are challenged to recognize, develop and share their gifts in an attempt to eradicate the evils of the world and bring salvation to all. The call to service is universal; no one is excluded or excused! In various ways and according to distinctive functions we all are involved in the teaching, worshipping and stewardship dimension of Jesus' Church. Our challenge is to be faithful and creative.

In a recent work on ministry, Fr. Schillebeeckx comments:

> Without doubt it is difficult to make a precise definition, or to locate exactly the relationship between salvation or Christian redemption and human liberation. But salvation and redemption which does not take any tangible form in our historical dimension seems to me to be tantamount to supernaturalism and ideology.[15]

This warning against a false dualism is to be taken seriously. Though we live with paradoxes (time/eternity; body/soul; mortality/immortality; freedom/limitation) we take these to be part of a dialectical process leading to growth and salvation. Our ministry and mission must straddle a variety of worlds and communities. The Church is wise and powerful enough to do this. In prayer and deep theological reflection, we are continually challenged to integrate the call to human liberation with a sense of the eschaton, to strive for justice/peace while keeping our eyes on things above, to plunge into the dustiness of life while embracing a contemplative stance. Though no one individual is likely to succeed, the Church as a community brings sufficient gifts and grace to accomplish the task.

THEME 8: EDUCATION

THESIS: *Christian education embraces a knowledge and practice of the Church's social teaching regarding economic and social affairs.*

Above all, we affirm that the social teaching proclaimed by the Catholic Church cannot be separated from her traditional teaching regarding man's life. Wherefore, it is our earnest wish that more and more attention be given to this branch of learning. First of all, we urge that attention be given to such studies in Catholic schools on all levels, and especially in seminaries, although we are not unaware that in some of these latter institutions this is already being done admirably.

Moreover, we desire that social studies of this sort be included among the religious materials used to instruct and inspire the lay apostolate, either in parishes or in associations. Let this diffusion of knowledge be accomplished by every modern means: that is, in journals, whether daily or periodical; in doctrinal books, both for the learned and the general reader; and finally, by means of radio and television. (222-223)

To be complete, the education of Christians must relate to the duties of every class. It is therefore necessary that Christians thus inspired, conform their behavior in economic and social affairs to the teachings of the Church. (228)

We do not regard such instruction [in the social teaching of the Church] as sufficient, unless there be added to the work of instruction that of the formation of man, and unless some action follow upon the teaching, by way of experience. (231)

In one of her short stories, Flannery O'Connor notes:

> She had managed after he died to get the two of them
> through college and beyond; but she had observed that
> the more education they got, the less they could do.[16]

The truth of this reflection is too accurate to be really humorous. Our increase in knowledge regarding political, economic and social philosophies of life can be so overwhelming that they paralyze both individuals and societies. The mind, laden with volumes of ideas and theories, suffers the same fate as that of any overtaxed and gluttonous appetite: inertia. Education's goal is quite different: a sensitivity and vision of life that elicits actions and concern. Norman Cousins says it well: "Respect for the fragility and importance of an individual life is still the first mark of the educated man."

Christian education, though embracing philosophical and theological understandings of reality, is not limited to the cognitive domain. Social teaching (that body of knowledge explicating the interrelationship between and among people in the economic, political and societal areas of life) must be communicated in intelligible ways and assimilated deep within the heart if the Church is to fulfill her task of building the kingdom of God. Such education is complex and difficult. Careful discernment and rigorous study are demanded. The challenge in our age causes some to despair of finding the truth or, the truth having been found, getting it into life in a practical fashion.

Business has a bottom line: profit! Analogously the social teaching of the Church has one as well: action! Education that does not ultimately have an impact on society and history is a failure. Jesus gave the disciples not only a vision but a mandate to live the truth in a community of persons. His vision of covenant provided the disciples with a frame of reference within which they could evaluate the values and activities of people and societies. His own example provided motivation and energy to enflesh the commandment of love. The gospel call, while being informative, is also formative. One author states: "I believe that the discovery of tastes is the essence of education more than filling the mind with information."[17] Three movements are implicit in a full Christian education: information, taste and action. The basic dynamic is one of invitation and imperative. Through invitation one is made aware of reality; through the imperative a challenge to conform one's life to reality through action is made explicit. "Ivory towers" may look nice but they fail to meet the people in dire need who circle around them. The social teachings of the Church present us with a vision and a call to action.

THEME 9: WORK
THESIS: *Work is a noble expression of the human person and has redemptive value when done in union with the Lord.*

> Whence it is, that if Christians are also joined in mind and heart with the most Holy Redeemer, when they apply themselves to temporal affairs, their work in a way is a continuation of the labor of Jesus Christ Himself, drawing from it strength and redemptive power: "He who abides in Me, and I in him, he bears much fruit." Human labor of this kind is so exalted and ennobled that it leads men engaged in it to spiritual perfection, and can likewise contribute to the diffusion and propagation of the fruits of the Redemption to others. (260)

> However, it is in full accord with the designs of God's providence that men develop and perfect themselves by exercise of their daily tasks, for this is the lot of practically everyone in the affairs of this mortal life. (256)

> He [Leo XIII] first and foremost stated that work, inasmuch as it is an expression of the human person, can

by no means be regarded as a mere commodity. For the great majority of mankind, work is the only source from which the means of livelihood are drawn. Hence, its remuneration is not to be thought of in terms of merchandise, but rather according to the laws of justice and equity. Unless this is done, justice is violated in labor agreements, even though they are entered into freely on both sides. (18)

A significant portion of every person's life is given to work. The meaning attached to this activity is of great import lest, unable to find a worthy purpose for this use of time and energy, a person despairs of making a significant contribution to the lives of others. The present encyclical explicitly acknowledges that work can be an expression of one's humanness and must never be treated as a mere thing, being purchased or sold regardless of the person. Work is part of God's plan and is an important means toward perfection. Nor does work accomplish this task by way of mere intention; the very work itself has an intrinsic worth that furthers creation.

Ideally, work should contribute to human fulfillment and the building of the kingdom, but actually, its effect on the lives of many can be vastly different. One contemporary author describes what happens when "workism" becomes an obsession:

> Work is what he thinks about. Work is his fix. The dividing line between work and private life is blurred early. He works at parties, in the shower, in his fitful early-waking dreams; he works even at play. The point of the vacation is to recharge his batteries for more work; the point of the golf game is to sew up a business friendship, unless the point of the game is even more basic: to win the championship.[18]

Such experiences indicate the divorce between the interiority of our lives and its expression in work. Compulsive competition controls one's life; productivity becomes both means and end; our culture determines our use of time; our identity is made synonymous with achievement. The social teaching of the Church preserves the nobility of the vocation to work with a demand that we balance our life with leisure, friendships and worship. Work is a part of the whole and has its rightful place. Detached and domineering work is a modern "golden calf" whose admirers are many, whose critics are few.

Certain forms of work do not of themselves challenge people to full human development. Putting labels on cans for eight hours a day, tightening nuts on bolts for forty hours a week, punching holes in leather for twenty-five years—none of these types of employment offers much creativity and in some instances much human contact. Other forms of work have the potential to stimulate and energize: teaching, tending the soil, artistic enterprises. Of the essence is the source from which our work flows:

> Before God, work that does not come from your (inmost) self is dead. . . . If a man's work is to live, it must come from the depths of him—not from alien sources outside himself— but from within.[19]

THEME 10: OBSTACLES TO JUSTICE AND PEACE

THESIS: *The obstacles to justice and peace are many: imbalanced sharing of goods; diametrically opposed concepts of life and the human person; a pervasive distrust rendering dialogue and sharing most difficult.*

> It is not easy for them [countries] to keep the peace advantageously if excessive imbalances exist in their economic and social conditions. (157)

> In this connection many systems of thought have been developed and committed to writing: some of these already have been dissipated as mist by the sun; others remain basically unchanged today; still others now elicit

less and less response from men. The reason for this is that these popularized fancies neither encompass man, whole and entire, nor do they affect his inner being. Moreover, they fail to take into account the weaknesses of human nature, such as sickness and suffering: weaknesses that no economic or social system, no matter how advanced, can completely eliminate. Besides, men everywhere are moved by a profound and unconquerable sense of religion, which no force can ever destroy nor shrewdness suppress. (213)

Although this [need for cooperation and mutual assistance] becomes more and more evident each day to individuals and even to all peoples, men, and especially those with high responsibility in public life, for the most part seem unable to accomplish the two things towards which peoples aspire. This does not happen because peoples lack scientific, technical, or economic means, but rather because they distrust one another. Indeed, men, and hence States, stand in fear of one another. One country fears lest another is contemplating aggression and lest the other seize an opportunity to put such plans into effect. Accordingly, countries customarily prepare defenses for their cities and homeland, namely, armaments designed to deter other countries from aggression. (203)

The fullness of the kingdom of God, a kingdom of justice and peace, will be realized only in the completeness of eternal life. Yet we are called now to promote that kingdom even though the detours and potholes are numerous. Greed and insensitivity lead to the imbalance of goods and opportunities. Certain theories of the human person and the meaning of life negate human dignity. Fears of every sort create an atmosphere of suspicion and distrust making mutuality and cooperation only dreams. Such obstacles must not deter us. Our challenge is to construct a sound philosophy and theology of life, to deepen trust regardless of the risk, to promote balance of goods among all peoples. In embracing that challenge the justice that overflows into peace is being realized now.

Candidness demands that each individual and every nation look into the mirror in an attempt to assess the quality of justice:

> Let us be honest, how deeply must we penetrate human nature before we strike greed and violence? Christ says: Greed and violence are also to be found in the wise man who teaches wisdom, in the preacher who preaches pity, in the teacher who educates, in the superior who commands, in the lawgiver who creates justice, in the judge who metes it out—in all of us! Only One is entirely free from them.[20]

Much of history can only be understood in terms of the relationship between greed and violence. What is acquired and claimed as one's own will be protected by means that at times become violent. An obvious problem arises. As fewer and fewer acquire more and more, greater defenses will be built up in a protective stance. The "have nots," deprived even of the basics of life, will not sit by and go unfed. The vicious circle of greed and violence accelerates and wars and riots break the order that is necessary for peace. It is no small wonder that Jesus preached poverty as the first beatitude and warned his disciples against the use of violence.

Theories are powerful. They influence the direction of our choices and how we relate to life and people. Underlying Nazi Germany, American slavery, religious bigotry are speculations of what the human person is and what life is all about. Some theories make justice and peace impossible because by definition they deny the human person a basic dignity, the foundation of justice and peace. Most family quarrels and international wars are the consequence of theories that fail to comprehend the essence of life. A distorted vision is like an arrow that leaves the bow off target—

each progressive inch of the flight leads to greater distortion and perversion.

Trust is the cornerstone of all human relating. Take away this precious gift, and fear, that ubiquitous human emotion, begins to dominate. Though certain forms of fear can promote healthy relating, most forms are destructive and alienating. Sadat speaks of the destructiveness of such fear:

> I have had the opportunity to observe that the gravest injustice done to the Egyptian people was the "cultivation of fear," that is, rather than trying to build up the inner man we did all we could to make him feel frightened. Fear is, I believe, a most effective tool in destroying the soul of an individual—the soul of a people.[21]

The encyclical calls for the "cultivation of trust" so that justice and peace can be realized. John XXIII has provided us with a magnificent vision. Our task will be to implement it.

Footnotes

1. Anwar el-Sadat, *In Search of Identity* (New York: Harper & Row 1977), 77.
2. *The Simone Weil Reader*, ed. George A. Panichas (New York: David McKay Company, Inc., 1977), 62.
3. Bernard Malamud, *The Fixer* (New York: Pocket Books, 1966), 234.
4. Avery Dulles, S.J., *Models of the Church* (New York: Doubleday & Company, 1978), 24.
5. Thomas Hardy, *The Return of the Native* (New York: The New American Library, 1959), 298.
6. Edward Schillebeeckx, *Ministry—Leadership in the Community of Jesus Christ* (New York: The Crossroads Publishing Co., 1981), 137.
7. Thomas Hardy, *The Return of the Native*, 390.
8. Anwar el-Sadat, *In Search of Identity*, 141.
9. G.K. Chesterton, *Orthodoxy* (New York: Doubleday Image Book, 1959), 95.
10. Goethe, *Faust*, trans. and introduction by Walter Kaufmann (New York: Anchor Books, Doubleday & Company, Inc., 1961), 469.
11. Hermann Hesse, *Steppenwolf*, trans. Hilda Rosner (New York: New Directions Publishing Corp., 1951), 53.

12. "Character" in *The Selected Writings of Ralph Waldo Emerson*, ed. Brooks Atkinson (New York: The Modern Library, 1940), 368.

13. Romano Guardini, *The Lord* (Chicago: Henry Regnery Company, 1954), 82.

14. Aldo Leopold, *A Sand County Almanac* (New York: Ballantine Books, Inc., 1966), 210.

15. Edward Schillebeeckx, *Ministry—Leadership in the Community of Jesus Christ*, 114.

16. "The Enduring Chill" in Flannery O'Connor's *The Complete Stories* (New York: Farrar, Straus and Giroux, 1971), 361.

17. Colman McCarthy, *Inner Companions* (Washington, D.C.: Acropolis Books Ltd., 1975), 17.

18. Gail Sheehy, *Passages* (New York: E.P. Dutton & Co., Inc., 1979), 223.

19. *Meister Eckhart*, trans. Raymond B. Blakney (New York: Harper Torchbooks, 1941), 244.

20. Romano Guardini, *The Lord*, 161.

21. Anwar el-Sadat, *In Search of Identity*, 209.

EVANGELII NUNTIANDI:
Themes and Theses

Pope Paul VI shared with the entire Church a demanding challenge when he issued his Apostolic Exhortation *Evangelii Nuntiandi* on December 8, 1975. The call to evangelize is no simple task. Add to this the complexity and pluralism of our time and the challenge may seem overwhelming. Yet God's grace is stronger than any human obstacle. With faith we realize that even though secularism and atheism are powerful influences on human consciousness, yet like a powerful magnet, the love of God made visible in Jesus continues to draw all people back to its true Origin. There are some positive forces aiding evangelization: the happy realization that religious experience and scientific expertise are not mutually exclusive, the long overdue dialogue between theology and culture, the new friendship between faith and reason. These hopeful events make evangelization a process that can truly transform human lives and our collective systems. The struggle is far from over; yet the goal is becoming clear and new means and methods are available to achieve our ends. With deep faith and firm commitment the Church can continue to fulfill her mission of proclaiming and bringing about the Kingdom of God.

The Apostolic Exhortation is rich in insight and vision.

This chapter focuses on ten themes that Pope Paul VI emphasizes in the hope of raising our consciousness and calling us to action. A thesis is drawn from each theme and is supported by three or more direct quotations from the text. Hopefully the reader will be drawn to the primary source and will ponder the document in active reflection. Following the supporting reference I offer a personal commentary that elaborates on the theme and thesis in light of historical experience. The commentary is more limited and restrictive than the main document.

Reading without reflection not only is a waste of time and energy but also is dehumanizing. It is not sufficient to take a posture of a sponge and simply absorb whatever knowledge is given. Reading demands study, criticism and prayer if new knowledge is to be internalized and integrated into life. Indeed knowledge that calls for action and does not lead to that natural fulfillment becomes injurious to one's psychic and spiritual health. Such a document as *Evangelii Nuntiandi* cannot be reflectively read and leave us the same as we were before. If it does, we have already died and are merely having a long wake.

THEME 1: EVANGELIZATION: ITS MEANING
THESIS: *Evangelization consists of many diverse but complementary elements, all of which proclaim the good news of God's love and his liberating salvation in Jesus Christ.*

> Evangelization, as we have said, is a complex process made up of varied elements: the renewal of humanity, witness, explicit proclamation, inner adherence, entry into the community, acceptance of signs, apostolic initiative. These elements may appear to be contradictory, indeed mutually exclusive. In fact they are complementary and mutually enriching. Each one must always be seen in relationship with the others. (24)

... to evangelize is first of all to bear witness, in a simple and direct way, to God revealed in Jesus Christ, in the Holy Spirit; to bear witness that in his Son God has loved the world—that in his Incarnate Word he has given being to all things and has called men to eternal life. (26)

... to proclaim with authority the Word of God, to assemble the scattered people of God, to feed this people with the signs of the action of Christ which are the Sacraments, to set this people on the road to salvation, to maintain it in that unity of which we are, at different levels, active and living instruments, and unceasingly to keep this community gathered around Christ faithful to its deepest vocation. And when we do all these things, within our human limits and by the grace of God, it is a work of evangelization that we are carrying out. (68)

Evangelization is about God encountering people. Zacchaeus perched in a tree and hearing the invitation of Jesus; the men of Athens attentively listening to the message of Paul; the dying person in Calcutta feeling the comforting touch of Mother Teresa; the prisoner visited by a chaplain; the mother or father lovingly nurturing a child to faith. Whenever and wherever the good news of God's love is proclaimed or witnessed to, the mysterious process of evangelization is taking place. Perhaps the message at times falls on deaf ears; perhaps the sharing of love brings about no noticeable change. Yet the fact remains that the kingdom of God is being preached in word and deed, and people in a unique way are given the gracious opportunity of encountering their God.

Evangelization is a dynamic process consisting of many components. Perhaps the most obvious one is proclamation: the explicit announcing of the mystery of God's love for us in Jesus. It is not sufficient for the message to be implicit; it must be spoken and told. An editorial in *America* provides an example:

But at his final A.F.L.-C.I.O. Convention last November George Meany did allow his faith an explicit expression as he said goodbye: "To God go my prayers of thanks for granting me more than one man's share of happiness and rewards, and prayers for His continued blessings on this nation and on this movement and on each of you."[1]

Proclamation of God's blessings reveals that evangelization is characterized by witness. Having experienced grace a person stands up and testifies in his or her words and life the goodness of God. The power unleashed for the renewal of people in this process cannot be described. How many lives have been radically altered through the witness of Augustine's *Confessions*, Teresa of Avila's *Interior Castle*, Isaiah's prophetic word. People are attracted to join the community of believers in Jesus because that community celebrates a new life in Christ. The process of evangelization must go full circle to be complete: those who witness the message of the good news must in turn stand before others and share the gift received.

A caution may well be in order. Evangelization can begin to go in the direction of religious concepts or theological interpretations which have great validity and importance: the notion of grace, the fact of sin, the mystery of the Church, the beauty of liturgy, the art of discernment, the role of authority, etc. Indeed, as we develop in faith a carefully worked out theology is essential. Yet concepts and theologies can be emphasized to such an extent that we miss the heart of evangelization: the person of Jesus and the kingdom he preached. Evangelization centers on the mystery and person of Christ Jesus who reveals the Father and the Spirit:

> There is no true evangelization if the name, the teaching, the life, the promises, the Kingdom and the mystery of Jesus of Nazareth, the Son of God are not proclaimed. (22)

St. Paul challenges us to put on the mind and heart of Christ Jesus. It is in this transformation that evangelization reaches its high point. Spiritual renewal moves from theory to fact, from a vague concept to an experienced reality, from a possibility to an actuality. It is not sufficient to merely hear or see or taste the goodness of the Lord; we must become, in our innermost being, true images of our Father's creative love. This applies both to us as individuals as well as to the whole of humanity; no one is exempt. Thus:

> For the Church, evangelizing means bringing the Good News into all the strata of humanity, and through its influence transforming humanity from within and making it new. (18)

THEME 2: HOLINESS

THESIS: *Evangelization is grounded in the power of the Holy Spirit who calls us to holiness and enables us to live in Christ.*

> The world calls for and expects from us simplicity of life, the spirit of prayer, charity towards all, especially the lowly and the poor, obedience and humility, detachment and self-sacrifice. Without this mark of holiness, our word will have difficulty in touching the heart of modern man. (76)

> It is therefore primarily by her conduct and by her life that the Church will evangelize the world, in other words, by her living witness of fidelity to the Lord Jesus—the witness of poverty and detachment, of freedom in the face of the powers of the world, in short, the witness of sanctity. (41)

> It must be said that the Holy Spirit is the principal agent of evangelization: it is he who impels each individual to proclaim the Gospel, and it is he who, in the depths of consciences, causes the word of salvation to be accepted and understood. But it can equally be said that he is the goal of evangelization: he alone stirs up the new crea-

> tion, the new humanity of which evangelization is to be
> the result, with that unity in variety which evangeliza-
> tion wishes to achieve within the Christian community.
> Through the Holy Spirit the Gospel penetrates to the
> heart of the world, for it is he who causes people to
> discern the signs of the times—signs willed by God—
> which evangelization reveals and puts to use within
> history. (75)

Without denying the power of words the primary moti-
vational force affecting our lives is a lived deed. By examin-
ing the behavior of people we come to see what their real
values are. Skepticism results when ideals are proclaimed
from the housetop while actual history records a different
story. The Church must live what she professes to be; the
Church must incarnate the love and forgiveness given her
by Christ. This happens when simplicity of life avoids the
entrapment of luxury, when the spirit of prayer grounds
our activity in God, when charity refuses to endorse any
form of discrimination, when self-sacrifice is characterized
by joy; then the world at large will be shocked from its
apathy and disbelief and will be challenged to consider an
alternative life style. The call to authenticity and holiness
demands our witnessing to Gospel values.

Evangelization does not happen without holiness; holiness is not possible without the gift of the Holy Spirit. The
document clearly states that it is the Spirit who impels us to
proclaim the good news, stirs people to respond, and pene-
trates the heart of the world. As in all ministries, we must
beware lest we lose sight of the source and goal of evangelization. The working of the Spirit, whose power we cannot
even imagine, is the gift offered by Jesus to a weary and
battered world. Openness to the Spirit draws us into the life
of God, the life of holiness. From this position of oneness,
we venture forth to share the life of grace with the entire
world. To attempt this work without that unity is certain

failure. Evangelization is not the work of human beings in its last analysis; rather, it is the work of God through us. Such instrumentality is a great and noble privilege.

While protecting the primacy of grace in the evangelization process, the Lord seeks our finite but important cooperation. A certain degree of human efficiency (task-orientation) and effectiveness (people-orientation) is essential. The efficient person gets the task done. Certain skills of communication, proper programming, understanding the psychological and spiritual development of persons are all important tools necessary to achieve the goal. Supplemented by a rich quality of prayer, an intense love and a willingness to sacrifice, a person comes to the task with developed grace and human skills. Effectiveness means that as we do our ministry we must be sensitive to people and where they are coming from. Evangelization that disregards the culture of a people—their customs and language, their history and limitations—will ultimately be a disservice both to them and to the gospel of Christ. We always evangelize in a historical context. Too often evangelizers have been efficient without being effective, e.g., enforced baptisms and whole nations blindly following the conversion of a single leader. At other times evangelizers were sensitive to people but lacked essential skills to do the task and fulfill the mission. People went away with distorted understanding and misguided formation. Though the Spirit is the source of holiness and the power behind evangelization, this faith fact does not exempt us from proper human development and training.

THEME 3: ADAPTATION AND FIDELITY

THESIS: *Evangelization demands the sensitivity of maintaining complete fidelity to the message of Jesus while adapting it to the circumstances of the people being evangelized.*

Evangelization loses much of its force and effectiveness if it does not take into consideration the actual people to whom it is addressed, if it does not use their language, their signs and symbols, if it does not answer the questions they ask, and if it does not have an impact on their concrete life. (63)

This fidelity both to a message whose servants we are and to the people to whom we must transmit it living and intact is the central axis of evangelization. (4)

On us particularly, the pastors of the Church, rests the responsibility for reshaping with boldness and wisdom, but in complete fidelity to the context of evangelization, the means that are most suitable and effective for communicating the Gospel message to the men and women of our times. (40)

Truly the effort for evangelization will profit greatly—at the level of catechetical instruction given at church, in the schools, where this is possible, and in every case in Christian homes—if those giving catechetical instruction have suitable texts, updated with wisdom and competence, under the authority of the Bishops. The methods must be adapted to the age, culture, and aptitude of the persons concerned: they must seek always to fix in the memory, intelligence and heart the essential truth that must impregnate all of life. (44)

During the past fifteen to twenty years the Church has made new and bold attempts to renew herself and to reach out to all people with the good news of salvation. A constant struggle has continued within that complex process to maintain without compromise what is essential to the faith while at the same time to let go willingly of historical and culturally conditioned expressions and formulations. The results have been mixed: some successes and some failures. The distinction between what is essential and what is accidental has been blurred at times; certain groups have refused to change traditional ritual practices while others have rejected outright any structure and form; polarization among theologians has raised havoc for the common person who becomes bewildered when the "doctors" disagree. Thus it comes as no surprise that the present document is extremely sensitive to the question of fidelity to the Gospel message while demanding proper adaptation in communicating doctrine to the people. The delicate balance challenges the teaching and preaching Church.

The central mysteries of our faith—creation, sin, covenant, incarnation, redemption, resurrection, ascension, pentecost—reveal the mystery of God's love and concern for us. The good news of salvation must be proclaimed in its totality, it must be a gospel without compromise. Our individual and collective memories must store these treasures and their development through tradition and history. Our treasury is great, yet so unknown. Cardinal Newman expressed a concern in the nineteenth century which applies to our own:

We [Catholics] have a vast inheritance, but no inventory of our treasures. All is given us in profusion; it remains for us to catalogue, sort, distribute, select, harmonize, and complete. We have more than we know how to use; stores of learning but little that is precise and serviceable; Catholic truth and individual opinion, first principles and the guesses of genius, all mingled in the same works, and requiring to be discriminated. We meet with truths overstated or misdirected, matters of detail variously taken, facts incompletely proved or applied, and rules inconsistently urged or discordantly interpreted. Such indeed is the state of every deep philosophy in its first stages, and therefore of theological knowledge. What we need at present for our Church's wellbeing, is not invention, nor originality, nor sagacity, nor even learning in our divines, at least in the first place, though all gifts of God are in a measure needed, and never can be unseasonable when used religiously, but we need peculiarly a sound judgment, patient thought, discrimination, a comprehensive mind, an abstinence from all private fancies and caprices and personal tastes, in a word, Divine Wisdom.[2]

Our imaginations must be as creative as our memories are accurate. The message must be reshaped so as to "fit" the mind, hearts and culture of our day. We must address ourselves to the questions that ravish the hearts of people. What is the meaning of life and death? What is my personal role in history? Is love possible for our times? How can justice and peace be achieved in an age of violence and disrespect? Our faith helps us to provide meaning and insight into these basic questions. How our faith is expressed, the language, signs and symbols that we use, must be such as to foster, not hinder the sharing of truth. Recognition of theological illiteracy among many of our people needs to be confronted and every effort made to overcome this sad fact. The message must touch the concrete lives of people and institutions; otherwise it turns into pure theory and is blown away by the wind. People know immediately, from the tone of voice and the words chosen and examples given whether or not the evangelizer lives on planet earth. Boldness is called for, wisdom is needed, skills in communication are essential. We might be consoled by this fact: if the mission has been given us we can be assured of the necessary graces to accomplish it.

A trend might be noted. More and more people are moving in the direction of video-audio techniques. The written/printed word has less influence on the lives of people than it once did. If this phenomenon continues to manifest itself, we must adapt our methods accordingly. The delivery system is conditioned upon the communication style of a given people; the message is unconditional and radically the same. This is a vital concern for anyone who takes evangelization seriously.

THEME 4: INTERIOR RENEWAL

THESIS: *Evangelization seeks to transform the mind and heart of each individual and of all humankind, making them into the likeness of the Lord Jesus.*

> But above all each individual gains them [kingdom and salvation] through a total interior renewal which the Gospel calls *metanoia*; it is a radical conversion, a profound change of mind and heart. (10)

> The Church considers it to be undoubtedly important to build up structures which are more human, more just, more respectful of the rights of the person and less oppressive and less enslaving, but she is conscious that the best structures and the most idealized systems soon become inhuman if the inhuman inclinations of the human heart are not made wholesome, if those who live in these structures or who rule them do not undergo a conversion of heart and of outlook. (36)

> The purpose of evangelization is therefore precisely this interior change, and if it had to be expressed in one sentence the best way of stating it would be to say that the Church evangelizes when she seeks to convert, solely through the divine power of the Message she proclaims, both the personal and collective consciences of people, the activities in which they engage, and the lives and concrete milieux which are theirs. (18)

Chesterton's warning about how to maintain what is essential should be heeded:

> The unpopular parts of Christianity turn out when examined to be the very props of the people. The outer ring of Christianity is a rigid guard of ethical abnegations and professional priests; but inside that inhuman guard you will find the old human life dancing like children, and drinking wine like men; for Christianity is the only frame for pagan freedom. But in the modern philosophy the case is opposite; it is its outer ring that is obviously artistic and emancipated; its despair is within.[3]

Outer change and extrinsic modification may simply be a surface reality; evangelization, by its very definitions, plumbs the depths and seeks change at the very core of life. Three areas become objects of major concern: (1) consciences of people—that sacred domain wherein values reside and from which actions flow; (2) activities—those words and deeds which bring into existence life or death; (3) environments—that territory and atmosphere that provides opportunities for growth or which stifle the seeds of human potential. This is big game; the stakes are high! Both information and formation are necessary. At times, reformation will be necessary. The focus of the interior renewal of evangelization is "form," that principle of life that demands shaping and molding. Christ is the model that provides the criteria for our efforts. Are we malleable enough to receive the imprint of his hand?

Resistance to this process of conversion should be expected. Every change demands a letting go, it involves a dying process. Our false self dies hard. It often is covered over with layers of defense mechanisms that make contact with God's word most difficult. Soon we realize how powerless we are with mere human efforts to change; we are forced to turn to God for his assistance. Renewal of mind and heart is a graced event. Though we act as instruments in some way, the work is primarily that of the Spirit. The Spirit proposes and disposes according to the Father's will.

Interior renewal focuses upon the individual; yet, by extension, also applies to systems and institutions. We speak of our corporations throughout the world as "corporate persons." Such writers as Jacques Ellul and Simone Weil express great concern regarding this emerging phenomenon. Prophetic voices speak out to warn us of the dangers inherent in individual responsibilities being turned over to anonymous boards of directors. Collective responsibility quickly tends to be no responsibility at all. The dignity of the individual will continue to be threatened until policies and programs of our large institutions are congruent with the dictates of justice and peace. The Church must play a prophetic and courageous role in this regard, criticizing whatever is not in accord with Gospel values and offering viable alternatives that bring new hope and life.

Interior renewal has a bottom line: kenosis. This self-emptying, modeled for us by Jesus who emptied himself and took on the form of our humanity, is a constant vocation in the conversion process. Our unspiritual self must die if we are to truly live. To give up resentments, to forego self-indulgent pleasures, to relinquish our vested interests, to shun the lure of avarice and false power—these challenges touch the roots of our being and are not eradicated without considerable pain and anguish. Yet there is no other way to holiness and wholeness. Evangelization, whose business is interior renewal, is concerned with the ultimate realities of life.

THEME 5: TRUTH AND STUDY

THESIS: *Evangelization demands constant study and prayer if truth is to be discovered and shared.*

> It is necessary above all to prepare good instructors— parochial catechists, teachers, parents—who are desirous of perfecting themselves in this superior art, which is indispensable and requires religious instruction. Moreover, without neglecting in any way the training of children, one sees that present conditions render ever more urgent catechetical instruction, under the form of the catechumenate, for innumerable young people and adults who, touched by grace, discover little by little the face of Christ and feel the need of giving themselves to him. (44)

> A serious preparation is needed for all workers for

evangelization. Such preparation is all the more necessary for those who devote themselves to the ministry of
the Word. Being animated by the conviction, ceaselessly
deepened, of the greatness and riches of the Word of
God, those who have the mission of transmitting it must
give the maximum attention to the dignity, precision
and adaptation of their language. Everyone knows that
the art of speaking takes on today a very great importance. How would preachers and catechists be able to
neglect this? (73)

Every evangelizer is expected to have a reverence for
truth, especially since the truth that he studies and com-
municates is none other than revealed truth and hence,
more than any other, a sharing in the first truth which is
God himself. The preacher of the Gospel will therefore
be a person who even at the price of personal renuncia-
tion and suffering always seeks the truth that he must
transmit to others. He never betrays or hides truth out of
a desire to please men, in order to astonish or to shock,
nor for the sake of originality or a desire to make an
impression. He does not obscure revealed truth by being
too idle to search for it, or for the sake of his own
comfort, or out of fear. He does not neglect to study it.
He serves it generously, without making it serve him.
(78)

The Bishops' Synod of 1974, which insisted strongly on
the place of the Holy Spirit in evangelization, also expressed the desire that pastors and theologians—and we
would also say the faithful marked by the sea of the
Spirit of Baptism—should study more thoroughly the
nature and the manner of the Holy Spirit's action in
evangelization today. This is our desire too, and we
exhort all evangelizers, whoever they may be, to pray
without ceasing to the Holy Spirit with faith and fervor
and to let themselves prudently be guided by him as the
decisive inspirer of their plans, their initiatives and their
evangelizing activity. (75)

For a variety of historical and sociological reasons, the

movement known as anti-intellectualism has gained many proponents in our time. Sad to say, many people who call themselves evangelists blatantly reject scholarship and serious study. Fundamentalistic and literal, they refuse to embrace basic principles of literary criticism and biblical scholarship. The disservice they do to God's word is extreme and tragic.

Scripture reveals the God of truth and the truths of God. In deep faith we accept the divine word and share it with others. To comprehend the truth contained in that word and to proclaim it accurately is no easy task. The tendency to filter out what is unpleasant, to slant passages so as to justify an attitude or practice, to color certain values to conform to our life style are strong urges within our frail personalities. Courage and brutal honesty are necessary to stand up in the light of God's truth. Our blind spots are many; our mindsets block clarity. Thus the present document calls us to the quality of reverence. We bow before God's truth regardless of what demands it makes in our lives. The prophets are models for us. They paid a great price in speaking the truth they heard: some were beaten, others excluded from their community, many were killed. Jesus proclaimed the truth and most people walked away. The light was too blinding, the challenges too threatening. Attached to the old and comfortable, the sacrifice to live in the truth and the freedom that truth brought was simply too great for most. They remained in darkness and slavery.

The autumn squirrel works diligently to extract the meat from the hickory nut. The Christian scholar who tries to break open the word of God must be persevering as well. Through meditation we ponder the scriptures; in faith we seek enlightenment. Study without prayer will easily lead to presumption; prayer without study may well keep us on the periphery of the central mysteries of our faith. Love for learning is not extremely popular within the Christian community. To that extent the process of evangelization suffers. Our understanding is limited unnecessarily; our communication is often incompetent and slipshod. The Lord has entrusted his word to us. One day an accounting will be due.

The ultimate goal of our study, prayer and evangelization is to discover the face of Christ and to give ourselves to his work in our time. Proper disposition becomes a significant ingredient in achieving this goal. Thus through preparation and study our minds and hearts are made ready for the truth; through cultivation of souls, others are made more receptive to the truth of God's word and can produce fruit, fruit that will last. Again a basic law of life applies: the autumn harvest is dependent upon the work done in the spring.

THEME 6: EVANGELIZERS

THESIS: *Evangelization, the essential mission of the Church, is the responsibility of every Christian; no one is exempt from this call and privilege.*

> The Second Vatican Council gave a clear reply to this question [but who then has a mission of evangelizing?]: it is upon the Church that "there rests, by divine mandate, the duty of going out into the whole world and preaching the Gospel to every creature." And in another text: ". . . the whole Church is missionary, and the work of evangelization is a basic duty of the People of God." (79)

> Those who sincerely accept the Good News, through the power of this acceptance and of shared faith, therefore gather together in Jesus' name in order to seek together the Kingdom, build it up and live it. They make up a community which is in its turn evangelizing. The command of the Twelve to go out and proclaim the Good News is also valid for all Christians, though in a different way. (13)

> Thus it is the whole Church that receives the mission to evangelize, and the work of each individual member is important for the whole. (15)
>
> Finally, the person who has been evangelized goes on to evangelize others. Here lies the test of truth, the touchstone of evangelization: it is unthinkable that a person should accept the Word and give himself to the Kingdom without becoming a person who bears witness to it and proclaims it in his turn. (24)

If Christian people were surveyed and asked if they saw themselves as evangelists, I am sure that most responses would be negative. This could be merely a problem of language. Evangelists, according to common usage, are the type that appear on television or hold tent meetings. Yet the problem is deeper than this, involving maturity and Christian self-understanding. The spreading of the good news and the building of the kingdom are seen by many baptized Christians as the tasks of a certain few: ordained ministers, religious, and perhaps a few laity—catechists, coordinators, teachers. The present document clarifies this misunderstanding: evangelization is the work of all baptized people. The gifts of God's life and love are to be shared. We cannot hoard them as unique possessions or accept them simply for our own well-being. We are called to pass them on by word, by example, by our very lives.

A basic problem may well stem from an inadequate ecclesiology. If the Church is perceived as essentially concerned with her own inner life, evangelization will not have high priority. However, if the outward thrust is duly appreciated and a sense of mission is highly developed, evangelization becomes a central concern. Further, if the Church is seen in terms of institution and hierarchy, then most people will shun any responsibility for the work of spreading the faith; it's someone else's job. Before evangelization will be accepted as a basic obligation and privilege for all, a tremendous amount of catechesis must be done. The missionary task of proclaiming God's love and forgiveness must be seen in a whole new perspective of the Church, that community of believers in Jesus who enter into his life and participate in his work. Acceptance of discipleship underlies the work of evangelization.

The call to carry on the work of evangelizing can be terribly threatening. Some fears may be quieted by recognizing the variety of roles and different functions in this universal ministry. Proclamation and witness have many faces. The public forum is one means, the kitchen table another. Eloquence will be demanded at times, but then a simple, kind word will fulfill the task in a different situation. Organizing and planning elicit the talents of some; letter writing and phone calls involve the gifts of others. What is crucial is involvement: we know the gift of faith we have received and we are committed to share it in some way with others. In fact, non-involvement is tantamount to a denial of our baptismal call.

Two characteristics are found in the authentic evangelizer: faith and joy. Faith leads us to the conviction that we are surrounded by God's redeeming love. Joy motivates us to share the good we possess, the life of grace. Perhaps evangelizers are lacking because of a want in faith or because joy is not intimately experienced. A deepening in both of these areas would lead to a more vibrant response to the basic mission of the Church.

THEME 7: ADHERENCE/COMMITMENT
THESIS: *Evangelization is rooted in personal adherence to Jesus Christ and the work of building the kingdom.*

Nevertheless the use of the means of social communication for evangelization presents a challenge: through

them the evangelical message should reach vast numbers of people, but with the capacity of piercing the
conscience of each individual, of implanting itself in his
heart as though he were the only person being addressed, with all his most individual and personal qualities, and evoke an entirely personal adherence and
commitment. (45)

In fact the proclamation only reaches full development
when it is listened to, accepted and assimilated, and
when it arouses a genuine adherence in the one who has
thus received it. An adherence to the truths which the
Lord in his mercy has revealed: still more, an adherence
to a program of life—a life henceforth transformed—
which he proposes. In a word, adherence to the Kingdom, that is to say the "new world," to the new state of
things, to the new manner of being, of living, of living in
community, which the Gospel inaugurates. Such an adherence, which cannot remain abstract and unincar-
nated, reveals itself concretely by a visible entry into a
community of believers. (23)

. . . the presentation of the Gospel message is not an
optional contribution for the Church. It is the duty
incumbent on her by the command of the Lord Jesus, so
that people can believe and be saved. This message is
indeed necessary. It is unique. It cannot be replaced. It
does not permit either indifference, syncretism or ac-
commodation. It is a question of people's salvation. It is
the beauty of the Revelation that it presents. It brings
with it a wisdom that is not of the world. It is able to stir
up by itself faith—faith that rests on the power of God. It
is truth. It merits having the apostle consecrate to it all
his time and all his energies, and to sacrifice for it, if
necessary, his own life. (5)

Every community has certain elements that constitute its
being. Three of these are awareness of origin and destiny,
acceptance of certain values and shared experience. The
Church and her work of evangelization demands all three

marks. We must know who we are and where we are going!
We are committed to a person and to a value system that is
clear and explicit! We are not an abstract group of people
gathered because of some lofty ideal or theory. Our coming
together flows from a shared experience of God's love and
forgiveness in Jesus. Thus the importance of adherence and
commitment become obvious in the work of evangelization.
Adherence means that we "cling" to Jesus as Lord; commitment means that we enter into the process of his life, death
and resurrection. The Paschal Mystery is the center of our
spiritual lives.

Our century is not terribly attracted to sustained relationships. In fact, many people doubt the possibility and
advisability of permanent relationships. Our faith provides
a different perspective. We believe in the covenant experience in which God first "adheres" to us his people in total
and absolute fidelity. At the center of his being is the word
"forever." In response our call is to freely accept his love and
mercy and thereby become his people. Relationships that
are authentic demand commitment. This commitment is
not merely of energy or time; it is a commitment of one's
very self. We give ourselves to the Lord who is by definition a
Self-Giver. Our commitment flows from a vision of the
kingdom and demands that the totality of our lives be sub-
mitted to God's reign. The issue here is serious and of
ultimate significance. Discipleship is costly and excludes
cheap grace in any form. Evangelization will not attract the
weak-hearted nor those unwilling to make a commitment.

Paradoxically, even those who refrain from accepting a
life of adherence and commitment cannot avoid the choice.
The human mind and heart is made to belong to someone
or something, to be committed to some person or thing. A
philosophy of non-adherence is adherence; a life style of
non-commitment is itself a commitment. Evangelization

presents an option: adhere to Jesus Christ and have eternal life, commit yourself to the Gospel and peace will be yours. Indeed, the cross will have its day, the gate will at times be small, the path, somewhat narrow. Yet the Lord is ever present with sufficient and sustaining grace. A great tragedy of history is that so many people have been evangelized in such a way that their adherence to a belief does not produce joy nor does their commitment become an adventure.

THEME 8: OBSTACLES

THESIS: *Evangelization will face resistance; two major forces in our day are secularism and atheism.*

In the course of twenty centuries of history, the generations of Christians have periodically faced various obstacles to this universal mission. On the one hand, on the part of the evangelizers themselves, there has been the temptation for various reasons to narrow down the field of their missionary activity. On the other hand, there has been the often humanly insurmountable resistance of the people being addressed by the evangelizer. (50)

This faith is nearly always today exposed to secularism, even to militant atheism. It is a faith exposed to trials, threats, and even more, a faith besieged and actively opposed. It runs the risk of perishing from suffocation or starvation if it is not fed and sustained each day. To evangelize must therefore very often be to give this necessary food and sustenance to the faith of believers, especially through a catechesis full of Gospel vitality and in a language suited to people and circumstances. (54)

Thus we have atheists and unbelievers on the one side and those who do not practice on the other, and both groups put up a considerable resistance to evangelization. The resistance of the former takes the form of a certain refusal and an inability to grasp the new order of things, and new meaning in the world, of life and of history; such is not possible if one does not start from a divine absolute. The resistance of the second group

> takes the form of inertia and the slightly hostile attitude
> of the person who feels that he is one of the family, who
> claims to know it all and to have tried it all and who no
> longer believes it. (56)

The sociologist Peter Berger speaks about the cognitive minority, i.e., a group of people in a given culture whose interpretation of human experience is not shared by the majority. This is the situation today for the Christian. The evangelizer must deal with people who have accepted an order of reality that is essentially sensate or rationalistic. The spiritual realm is rejected outright as medieval and archaic. Such concepts as sin and grace fail to find a reference point in reality. The atheist denies a transcendent being; the secularist is so preoccupied with the sensible world as to make religious questions irrelevant. Dr. Martin Marty in his excellent study *The Public Church* warns of the danger of underestimating the secular dimension of human experience: "Such an underestimation would seem on the face of it to be incredible to a thoughtful person who lives in the worlds of the higher academy, mass media of communication, literary and artistic culture, and commerce."[4] Here we see well-described the residence of secularism. In such an environment the God-reality confronts the constant refrain: "No room in the inn!" What can break through such a mighty fortress of secularism or the darkness of atheism? Some maintain that it takes tragedy, violent shock, war, personal illness, mental breakdown, endless anxiety. Perhaps the shock of love is powerful enough to commence the miraculous process of conversion.

Obstacles blocking evangelization can also come from within the Church. This happens when the Church fails to take seriously the outward mission of spreading the good news and instead turns in upon herself in stifling parochialism. Inbreeding can be deadly to the Christian spirit. Thus we find a strange phenomenon: people leaving the Church not by dropping out through the bottom but going out through the roof. The cause is often a type of suffocation when bitter infighting and petty jealousy over insignificant issues abound. The Gospel preached and the life lived within the Church fail to be expansive enough to embrace their energies. Then there are those individuals who were presented Catholic doctrine in ways that were too restrictive or distorted: Simone Weil felt that were she to join the Church she would be cutting herself off from the majority of humankind; James Joyce, in his autobiographical novel *A Portrait of the Artist as a Young Man*, proclaims his *non serviam* when presented with a God portrayed in horrendous colors; Emily Dickinson, though steeped in rich interiority and sensitivity, fled institutional religion because it failed to reverence the things of the spirit. Resistance to evangelization is not merely external, rooted in secularism and atheism. Blockage also comes from within through inaccurate theology and irreverent methodologies.

The Grand Inquisitor in Dostoevky's *The Brothers Karamazov* has Christ arrested because his preaching and life style is a threat to "the Church." Christ is calling people to freedom, to a life of love, to a radical poverty. But, according to the novel, what will happen to authority if freedom is lived; what will happen to all the accumulated wealth and power if people begin to truly love and live simply? Christ, for the good of the "Church," must be silenced. Dostoevsky describes well the resistance to the noble work of evangelization. Lack of interior reform makes the Church noncredible; lack of faith and openness without prevents the face of the true Christ from being discovered. Only the power of the Holy Spirit and a Church that is truly Christlike can overcome the obstacles blocking knowledge and love of God.

THEME 9: LIBERATION

THESIS: *Evangelization is concerned with the full liberation of people from all forms of oppression, especially from the oppression of sin.*

> As the kernel and center of his Good News, Christ proclaims salvation, this great gift of God which is liberation from everything that oppresses man but which is above all liberation from sin and the Evil One, in the joy of knowing God and being known by him, of seeing him, and of being given over to him. (9)

> But evangelization would not be complete if it did not take account of the unceasing interplay of the Gospel and of man's concrete life, both personal and social. This is why evangelization involves an explicit message, adapted to the different situations constantly being realized, about the rights and duties of every human being, about family life without which personal growth and development is hardly possible, about life in society, about international life, peace, justice and development — a message especially energetic today about liberation. (29)

> The Church, as the Bishops repeated, has the duty to proclaim the liberation of millions of human beings, many of whom are her own children—the duty of assisting the birth of this liberation, of giving witness to it, of ensuring that it is complete. This is not foreign to evangelization. (30)

Our history books sadly document centuries of oppression of every kind: slavery separating people from family and homeland, psychological bondage rooted in prejudice and violence; social, economic and religious chains holding captive millions of lives. Theologically we label this "sin." Sometimes it is the direct result of personal choice: often the political and cultural systems impede freedom. Whatever the cause, the suffering defies description.

Evangelization provides a message for such a history and

it is one of liberation. Jesus came to set people free from sin. All subhuman behavior became the object of his merciful but penetrating judgment. The dignity of every individual and the creative act of the Father were constant themes in the Lord's preaching. The Father's love was universal and salvific. Even Peter came to see that God shows no partiality!

Oppression can show its ugly face in any quarter. Though it is natural for us to turn to the blatant oppression of various political regimes, we must, in all honesty, face the oppressive attitudes and behavioral patterns that exist within our own community. Whenever responsible decision-making is denied, whenever authoritarian practices are employed, whenever power and wealth hold greater priority than persons, then confrontation must be made and the truth proclaimed. Hopefully, all the prophets are not dead. God calls forth special individuals to challenge the perennial danger of inculturation. Our task is to hear the voice of the Father in their words. When the message is shouted forth, we dare not feign ignorance nor deafness.

Liberation is not an unequivocal term; its meanings are many. The document expresses concern that we know which type of liberation we are speaking about:

> The Church links human liberation and salvation in Jesus Christ, but she never identifies them, because she knows through revelation, historical experience and reflection of faith that not every notion of liberation is necessarily consistent and compatible with an evangelical vision of man, of things and of events; she knows too that in order that God's kingdom should come it is not enough to establish liberation and to create well-being and development. (35)

Salvation is a much more comprehensive reality than liberation but it does embrace the fact of freedom from sin. While not down-playing the function of liberation, we must deal with its limitations.

Evangelization's ultimate test lies in action. We, who profess to be followers of the Lord Jesus, must move from principles of justice and peace into their concrete implementation. We liberate people from oppression by promoting and protecting their rights. Thus evangelization is highly pragmatic, demanding of us commitment and sacrifice. If the Gospel is truly proclaimed and lived, then the lives of individuals are freer and our systems are changed in such a way as to respect every individual. Only when the uniqueness of individuals is honored and their dignity carefully safeguarded will authentic liberation through evangelization be realized.

As Moses led the Hebrews out of slavery, and as Jesus, the new Moses, brought liberation from sin and death through the cross and resurrection, so too the Church must continue this same mission of freedom in the world today. This task will face many obstacles and encounter numerous distractions. We must not yield. Without freedom the human person cannot realize the full growth that God wills. Without freedom we live in fear that paralyzes the currents of grace within our minds and hearts. St. Paul, himself once enslaved in so many ways, championed the cause of liberation by proclaiming the freedom of the children of God. We witness to the same message and ministry.

THEME 10: HOPE

THESIS: *Evangelization relies on a promise of Presence and thus is characterized by a profound hope.*

> On the morning of Pentecost she [Mary] watched over with her prayer the beginning of evangelization prompted by the Holy Spirit: may she be the Star of the evangelization ever renewed which the Church, docile to her Lord's command, must promote and accomplish, especially in these times which are difficult but full of hope. (82)

. . . evangelization cannot but include the prophetic proclamation of a hereafter, man's profound and definitive calling, in both continuity and discontinuity with the present situation: beyond time and history, beyond the transient reality of this world, and beyond the things of this world, of which a hidden dimension will one day be revealed—beyond man himself, whose true destiny is not restricted to his temporal aspect but will be revealed in the future life. Evangelization therefore also includes the preaching of hope in the promises made by God in the new Covenant of Jesus Christ, the preaching of God's love for us and of our love for God; the preaching of brotherly love for all men—the capacity of giving and forgiving, of self-denial, of helping one's brother and sister—which, springing from the love of God, is the kernel of the Gospel: the preaching of the mystery of evil and of the active search for good. (28)

And may the world of our time, which is searching, sometimes with anguish, sometimes with hope, be enabled to receive the Good News not from evangelizers who are dejected, discouraged, impatient or anxious, but from ministers of the Gospel whose lives glow with fervor, who have first received the joy of Christ, and who are willing to risk their lives so that the Kingdom may be proclaimed and the Church established in the midst of the world. (80)

In the Vatican II document *Gaudium et Spes* we are presented with the Church's self-understanding that has brought her to identify so clearly her mission to the modern world:

The joys and the hopes, the griefs and the anxieties of the men of this age, especially those who are poor or in any way afflicted, these too are the joys and hopes, the griefs and anxieties of the followers of Christ. Indeed, nothing genuinely human fails to raise an echo in their hearts. For theirs is a community composed of men. United in Christ, they are led by the Holy Spirit in their journey to the Kingdom of their Father and they have welcomed the news of

> salvation which is meant for every man. That is why this
> community realizes that it is truly and intimately linked with
> mankind and its history. (1)

This magnificent passage is closely connected to the
present document on evangelization in that both seek to
bring hope to a weary and exhausted world. There is no
romanticism in either document. Hope is proclaimed in an
age that is marked with universal anxiety, horrendous violence and a pervasive sense of meaninglessness. Thus we
find people running to any "prophet" who seems to offer
the slightest freshness and hope.

Behind every hope is a vision of reality. The Church
boldly proclaims an eschatological picture that transcends
time and space. Naturalism and various forms of existentialism are systems of thought and life radically different
from the Christian perspective. All systems of meaning have
some form of hope, Christianity presents a large and eternal
Hope. That Hope confronts the fact of sin and deals with
the mystery of evil; it is a Hope that flows from a faith vision.
Unlike rationalism and secular humanism that are overwhelmed when finite reason comes up against sin and evil,
Christianity relies on the person of Jesus to guide us
through the maze of these mysteries. The Church looks to
the stars knowing of the loving presence of God and yet
deals with the muddiness of life following in the footsteps of
the Master. Faith and reason both find a home in the
Church; neither the *ought* nor the *is* is excluded; time and
eternity are loci for encountering the living and true God.
Evangelization deals with reality and in that search instills
hope.

If evangelization is so hope-filled, why have the dry
bones not come to life? Why has the preaching of the Gospel
not transformed more lives and infected more people with

joyful hope? Motivation demands fervor! Delight and zeal move people! A hope-filled person can persuade and change nations. The apostolic exhortation expresses a deep and pervasive concern: lack of fervor among those who carry the message. Who would respond to a message that flows from a discouraged spirit? Should we be surprised if people remain apathetic when preaching is wanting in joy or there is a buried note of anger and impatience coloring the words and the atmosphere? The manner of delivery and the content of the message should bring life and hope, not death and discouragement. Evangelization is greatly hampered when negativity and hopelessness infect the ministry of the word or various forms of service. The fires need to be rekindled time and time again. Prayer, support and large doses of affirmation would be of considerable help.

God has made a promise. Herein lies the foundation of our hope. He is with us and in us and for us—the promise of presence. He is working always within and among us, his people. God has a dream; can it be deferred?

What happens to a dream deferred?

Does it dry up
like a raisin in the sun?

Or fester like a sore—
And then run?

Does it stink like rotten meat?
Or crust and sugar over—
like a syrupy sweet?

Maybe it just sags
like a heavy load.

Or does it explode?

Langston Hughes (1902-1967)

Evangelization is about dreaming the possible dream. Our mission is to get on with the task and to share the good news with the whole world. God will realize his plan and we are privileged to be called to be instruments of his truth, peace and love.

Footnotes

1. *America* (January 26, 1980), 53.
2. John Henry Newman, *Apologia Pro Vita Sua* (Boston: The Riverside Press Cambridge, 1956), 82.
3. G.K. Chesterton, *Orthodoxy* (New York: Doubleday Image Books, 1959), 157.
4. Martin Marty, *The Public Church: Mainline—Evangelical—Catholic* (New York: Crossroad, 1981), 5.

REDEMPTOR HOMINIS:
Themes and Theses

On March 4th, 1979, Pope John Paul II shared with the world a document rich in insight and frought with consequences. His first encyclical, *Redemptor Hominis*, expressed many doctrines that are central not only to Christian life, but to the very meaning of human existence. It is a letter calling us to trust and risk, an epistle challenging us to regain our focus and to center on what is essential, a document that contains a philosophy-theology of the human person that is incredibly respectful of every individual and appreciative of human freedom and responsibility. It is a message that demands both careful study and quiet prayer.

This chapter culls out ten recurring themes that permeate the encyclical. Pondering the themes leads to a basic statement (thesis) that summarizes a truth or truths about the theme and attempts in a concise form to articulate a central message. Each theme and thesis is followed by some direct quotations from the document. Finally, I add my own reflections, commenting on what I personally think are implications or contiguous thoughts. These are personal and reflect my own observations only.

My purpose is to entice the reader to pick up the encyclical and to read it thoroughly and carefully, several times if possible. Too often these documents are not given sufficient attention resulting in a costly loss to our faith consciousness.

Pope John Paul II, already having deeply left his influence on so many of us, deepens that influence by sharing so masterfully his vision of Jesus, the redeemer of all people.

THEME 1: JESUS
THESIS: *Jesus Christ is the center of history and the key truth of our faith.*

> We . . . recall and reawaken in us in a special way our awareness of the key truth of faith which St. John expressed at the beginning of his Gospel: "The Word became flesh and dwelt among us," and elsewhere: "God so loved the world that he gave his only Son, that whoever believes in him should not perish but have eternal life." (1)

> Our spirit is set in one direction; the only direction for our intellect, will and heart is—toward Christ our redeemer, toward Christ, the redeemer of man. (7)

> Jesus Christ is the stable principle and fixed center of the mission that God himself has entrusted to man. (11)

Christianity has the appearance of great complexity: hundreds of doctrines, multiple forms of moral codes, volumes of rituals telling of ways to celebrate. Underlying these truths, moral standards and cultic rites is a person, the person of Jesus Christ. He is the visible sign of the Father's love; he is the eternal Son through whom all creation was brought forth; he is the one sent to reconcile all creation back to the Father; he is the one who suffered-died-rose in accord with the Father's plan; he is the one who, with the Father, sent their Spirit to form a Church, a community of love and forgiveness. Jesus is the central focus of the encyclical because he is the central point of history. All the truths of our faith find meaning and relevance in the light of Christ Jesus, the Lord.

Frequently in the encyclical, Pope John Paul II states

that he shares his personal thoughts and feelings: "When therefore at the beginning of the new pontificate I turn my thoughts and my heart to the redeemer of man, I thereby wish to enter and penetrate into the deepest rhythm of the Church's life." (22) There is a profound existential ring to the pattern—Jesus is not just someone known by the mind through faith but someone who has touched our hearts and stirred them into living flames. Jesus is both the central truth of our faith and the primary resident in our hearts. Because of his very person, we are transformed interiorly and this renewal finds expression in a new form of life style. Christianity is thus grounded in personal relationships: through the Son of God and in the Spirit, we come to the Father to share in the fullness of life.

The mystery of the incarnation draws our loving attention to the person of Jesus. Herein we see that God, in Jesus, takes on our human condition, becomes part and parcel of our history, accepts the suffering and death that is the fate of all mortal creation. God has visited his people in his Son, bringing us to freedom and grace. Further, ". . . by his incarnation, he, the Son of God, in a certain way united himself with each man." (8) It is precisely this union that provides the foundation for our worth and dignity. Though objectively this has taken place, each of us is challenged to experience this mysterious union within our own hearts and minds. Not to do so means to live in darkness; it is not to be aware of the good news.

With the coming of Jesus, all of history takes on new meaning. Cultures and civilizations are evaluated in the light of his person; movements and philosophies express truth only if they accord with his vision; destinies and fates are determined by means of his values and life style. Our faith provides a vision that allows for such interpretation and our faith centers on the person of the Lord. Without

Jesus Christ there is no way out of the maze of eternal questions that haunt the mind and heart of all of us; indeed, without Jesus, there is "No Exit"!

THEME 2: REDEMPTION

THESIS: *Redemption, the renewing of creation, is the mystery of how the Father has saved us in and through his Son, Jesus.*

> The redeemer of the world! In him has been revealed in a new and more wonderful way the fundamental truth concerning creation to which the Book of Genesis gives witness when it reports several times, "God saw that it was good." The good has its source in wisdom and love. In Jesus Christ the visible world which God created for man—the world that, when sin entered, "was subjected to futility"—recovers again its original link with the divine source of wisdom and love. Indeed, "God so loved the world that he gave his only Son." As this link was broken in the man Adam, so in the man Christ it was reforged. (8)

> The mystery of the redemption of the world—this tremendous mystery of love in which creation is renewed—is, at its deepest root, the fullness of justice in a human heart—the heart of the firstborn Son—in order that it may become justice in the hearts of many human beings, predestined from eternity in the firstborn Son to be children of God and called to grace, called to love. (9)

> Unceasingly contemplating the whole of Christ's mystery, the Church knows with all the certainty of faith that the redemption that took place through the cross has definitively restored his dignity to man and given back meaning to his life in the world, a meaning that was lost to a considerable extent because of sin. And for that reason, the redemption was accomplished in the paschal mystery, leading through the cross and death to resurrection. (10)

A powerful image is used here to depict a profound

mystery: redemption is like the restoration of a broken chain that connected God with his people. Sin broke the chain; Jesus has come to be the very link that re-connects the Father and creation. It is as if God were a blacksmith, reforging and remaking creation in a new way. William Blake, in marveling at the powerful maker of the tiger, writes:

> What the hammer? What the chain?
> Knit thy strength and forged thy brain?
> What the anvil? What dread grasp
> Dare its deadly terrors clasp?   (from "The Tiger")

We, too, marvel at the making anew of creation; and redemption was good, it was very good!

Though focusing on redemption, our faith necessarily embraces in one sweeping breath the other life mysteries as well: creation, incarnation, resurrection, pentecost. Through Jesus the Father made all things; in Jesus the Father's love takes on full visibility; by means of his obedience, Jesus is raised up by the Father, the firstborn of all creation; with Jesus, the Father sends their Spirit to transform and to continue to renew the earth. Redemption is understood in this context. Sin broke what was intended to be unified; redemption, in Jesus, was the mystery to re-establish that oneness that alone brings peace and joy.

The price of redemption was the cross and death. Love is always tested by the quality of one's willingness to suffer for the beloved. The Father loved creation so much that he freely gave his only Son for its salvation. The cross is a symbol of the destructiveness of sin; it is also the measure of divine love. Redemption further deals with an enigma that haunts the human spirit—the constant consciousness of mortality. The human person is powerless in the face of death, causing a fear seldom adequately described. In Jesus, the redeemer, sin and death have been broken. With John Donne we can boldly now say:

Death, be not proud, though some have called thee
Mighty and dreadful, for thou art not so;
For those whom thou think'st thou dost overthrow
Die not, poor Death; not yet canst thou kill me.

(from "Death")

The busyness of daily life tends to blot out the felt need for redemption. Caught up in our active lives, the sense of sin and the break in the chain of love does not get sufficient attention. We need but quiet our minds and hearts and hands for only a short time to realize the extent and destructiveness of sin. Denial of basic human rights, multiple forms of manipulation and exploitation, the subtle forms of selfishness, the blatant hatreds and devastating prejudices—at the end of a much lengthier litany we come to a single conclusion: "Father, have mercy on us; save us from our sins; heal and restore our broken hearts and lives!" In Jesus, our litany is already answered, we need but pray it in faith and live the Father's call:

This is what Yahweh asks of you:
only this, to act justly,
to love tenderly
and to walk humbly with your God.   (Micah 6:8)

THEME 3: THE HUMAN PERSON

THESIS: *Every individual has a dignity and value that provides ultimate meaning for life; that dignity and worth is grounded in one's union with Christ.*

Man cannot live without love. He remains a being that is incomprehensible for himself, his life is senseless, if love is not revealed to him, if he does not encounter love, if he does not participate intimately in it. This, as has already been said, is why Christ the Redeemer "fully reveals man to himself." If we may use the expression, this is the "human dimension" of the mystery of redemption. In this dimension man finds again the greatness, dignity and value that belong to his humanity. (10)

However, we can and must immediately reach and display to the world our unity in proclaiming the mystery of Christ, in revealing the divine dimension and also the human dimension of the redemption, and in struggling with unwearying perseverance for the dignity that each human being has reached and can continually reach in Christ, namely the dignity of both the grace of divine adoption and the inner truth of humanity, a truth which—if in the common awareness of the modern world it has been given such fundamental importance— for us is still clearer in the light of the reality that is Jesus Christ. (11)

The "price" of our redemption is likewise further proof of the value that God himself sets on man and of our dignity in Christ. (20)

Humanistic psychology has emphasized the worth of the human person in powerful terms and with strong reasoning. Certain forms of Christianity can be justly accused of failing to appreciate the dignity of the person. Pope John Paul II makes clear beyond any doubt the position of the Catholic Church, assigning to every individual divine worth because of union with Christ.

The test and touchstone for all of us as to whether or not we truly value others and ourselves is love. Being loved by God indelibly marks us as precious; being loved by our redeemer makes us great; being loved by the Spirit makes us temples, demanding utmost reverence and respect; being loved by one another confirms and enhances our value. Thus, the Holy Father cries out in anguish when love is replaced by hatred:

Do not kill! Do not prepare destruction and extermination for men! Think of your brothers and sisters who are suffering hunger and misery! Respect each one's dignity and freedom! (16)

The encyclical is timely in its call to value the dignity of each person. Research in psychology and sociology shows that many people do not hold themselves in proper esteem. A poor self-image is the oversimplistic term used. It is deeper than that. Meaninglessness, ennui and pure, unadulterated confusion about self and the world characterize our times. In such an environment, what a welcomed breeze to hear once again the significance and importance of every individual life. Life is not cheap; it has been purchased at a very great cost! Persons are not numbers; they are "immortal diamonds" seeking to be transparent to God's light and love. Existence is not meaningless; it is rich in mystery and permeated with the Spirit of the Father and Jesus. Gerard Manley Hopkins, though keenly aware of the scars and bruises of creation, could write with clear insight and a reverent hope:

> And for all this, nature is never spent;
>   There lives the dearest freshness deep down things;
> And though the last lights of the black West went,
>   Oh, morning, at the brown brink eastward, springs—
> Because the Holy Ghost over the bent
>   World broods with warm breast and with ah! bright wings.
>   (from "God's Grandeur")

The source of our dignity demands careful consideration. Does our value flow from superior intelligence; is our dignity grounded in our marvelous achievements, our transforming the earth; or is our worth rooted in certain forms of altruism that enrich the lives of others? The encyclical states:

> In reality, the name for that deep amazement at man's worth and dignity is the Gospel, that is to say: the good news. (10)

The good news is Jesus, his life-death-resurrection. Our dignity stems from our being enabled to participate in the paschal mystery, thereby sharing in the love, poverty and obedience of our Lord. We lose our dignity, and thus our self-esteem, by attempting to move beyond the reach of our Father's love in Jesus. The conclusion here is sad and not unlike the reflection by Gloucester in Shakespeare's *King Lear*:

> As flies to wanton boys are we to th' gods;
> They kill us for their sport. (IV, 1, 35)

THEME 4: THE HUMAN CONDITION

THESIS: *The Church must speak to our times, sensitive to contemporary needs, problems and possibilities.*

> Since this man is the way for the Church, the way for her daily life and experience, for her mission and toil, the Church of today must be aware in an always new manner of man's "situation." (14)

> Accordingly while keeping alive in our memory the picture that was so perspicaciously and authoritatively traced by the Second Vatican Council, we shall try once more to adapt it to the "signs of the times" and to the demands of the situation, which is continually changing and evolving in certain directions. (15)

> If therefore our time, the time of our generation, the time that is approaching the end of the second millennium of the Christian era, shows itself a time of great progress, it is also seen as a time of threat in many forms for man. The Church must speak of this threat to all people of good will and must always carry on a dialogue with them about it. Man's situation in the modern world seems indeed to be far removed from the objective demands of the moral order, from the requirements of justice, and even more of social love. (16)

Principles must be applied to specific situations; our faith must be spoken and proclaimed in a particular historical context. The Church of medieval times faced political, economic and provincial problems far different from our own. Though the same basic faith facts and moral guidelines apply now as in previous centuries, the context has so radically changed in intensity and extension that much confusion is upon us. Be that as it may, we must assume the responsibility of looking at the human condition in our times: a condition that contains the possibility of total annihilation, a situation of tremendous potential for progress or destruction, a moral milieu that demands high levels of responsibility and yet leaves freedom undefined. Our times are rich and laden with power; the question is: how will it be used?

Adaptation is a difficult art, demanding a firmness of principle with a high level of flexibility regarding forms, styles and expression. The process of change and updating is painful. Many desire to hang on to old forms as if they were of the essence. Others, in seeking to renew, forego principles in order to be falsely relevant. The balance is delicate and not without risk. One thing is certain, however: unless our faith is addressed to people in the real context of their lives, we are talking to no one. People will turn for meaning and solace to occult religions or transitory philosophies which, although often false and incomplete, at least attempt to speak to people where they are.

The encyclical calls us to dialogue, a theme that was powerfully and brilliantly addressed in Pope Paul VI's *Ecclesiam Suam*. Communication is essential to come to an understanding of what lies within the hearts and minds of people. Openness, willingness to learn and mutual respect are elements fostering honest exchange. Pope John Paul II proposes a basic guideline for dialogue:

> It is a noble thing to have a predisposition for understanding every person, analyzing every system and recognizing what is right; this does not at all mean losing certitude about one's

own faith or weakening the principles of morality, the lack of which will soon make itself felt in the life of whole societies, with deplorable consequences besides. (6)

Such a dialogue enters into every realm: family life, political movements, economic theories, military tactics, medical practices, artistic dreams and expressions, technological propositions, international controversy, futuristic planning, religious issues. Nothing is foreign to the concern of the Church because nothing that involves people can be disregarded. The Church must imbue each arena of life with its love and mission. Dialogue gets us in touch with the people and their lives; the Spirit confirms or challenges according to the matter at hand.

Jesus assumed the human condition in the incarnation. He spoke to the people in the context of their lives, sensitive to cultural concerns and open to their problems, their dreams and their expectations. He adapted his style to the person addressed; his message of love and forgiveness pierced every form and style of life. We can do no better than to follow his example.

THEME 5: TRUST

THESIS: *Though surrounded by difficulties and tasks, we must trust that the Lord will provide whatever we need.*

> It was to Christ the redeemer that my feelings and thoughts were directed on Oct. 16 of last year, when, after the canonical election, I was asked: "Do you accept?" I then replied: "With obedience in faith to Christ, My Lord, and with trust in the mother of Christ and of the Church, in spite of the great difficulties, I accept." (2)

> Can we fail to have trust—in spite of all human weakness and all the faults of past centuries—in our Lord's grace as revealed recently through what the Holy Spirit said and we heard during the council? (6)

> . . . in the sacramental sign he entrusts himself to us with
> limitless trust, as if not taking into consideration our
> human weakness, our unworthiness, the force of habit,
> routine, or even the possibility of insult. (20)

A word used to capture a common experience in the
twentieth century is *angst*. This worry, anxiety, troubledness
flows from our historical situation: world wars, rampant
exploitation, cultural rootlessness, racial bigotry, religious
indifference, unequal distribution of world resources, violence beyond description, political corruption, economic
manipulation. Amidst such activity there arises a sense of
hopelessness and despondency. Loss of faith in God results
in a loss of faith in ourselves. We begin to worry about our
worries, entering into the pitiable condition of phobo-
phobia!

Trust is much needed in such an environment, a trust
that is well-founded on a providential God. The scriptures
are replete with this call:

> Yahweh is my light and my salvation,
>   whom need I fear?
> Yahweh is the fortress of my life,
>   of whom should I be afraid? (Ps 27:1)

> Do not let your hearts be troubled.
> Trust in God still, and trust in me. (Jn 14:1)

> Nothing therefore can come between us and the love of
> Christ, even if we are troubled or worried, or being
> persecuted, or lacking food or clothes, or being threatened
> or even attacked. As scripture promised: For your sake we
> are being massacred daily, and reckoned as sheep for the
> slaughter. These are the trials through which we triumph,
> by the power of him who loved us. (Rm 8:35-37)

Pope John Paul II experienced in his life many of the
trials which St. Paul describes. He knew the agony and

terror of pain; yet, relying on the goodness and fidelity of God, he trusted that the Lord would give sufficient strength to fight or to endure. The events of the Second World War, the curtailment of human and religious freedoms under the communist regime, the personal suffering from the loss of loved ones all add tremendous weight to his call to trust in God. In the encyclical he writes:

> . . . I intend to continue, in a certain sense together with John Paul I, into the future, letting myself be guided by unlimited trust in and obedience to the Spirit that Christ promised and sent to his Church. (2)

Trust is based on a promise and draws its strength from the personal presence of God who dwells within us and the Church. Implicit here is a warning that we do not separate ourselves from the Lord—a separation that comes when we no longer communicate with God through prayer or that results from a life style that contradicts the Gospel values. In both instances, we leave the light for darkness. In that darkness our human weakness comes to the fore and we are overwhelmed by inadequacy and inferiority. We need trace but a few miles of history to see the results: arrogant imperialism, mental illness, broken hearts. In spite of all the limitations and weaknesses, in spite of all the insensitivity and coarseness, in spite of all our personal and collective sin, the Spirit of God still permeates the world seeking to be transparent through our lives. Trust allows that transparency; distrust throws us back on our isolated selves.

The tone of the encyclical is optimistic; it is also realistic. Our optimism comes from a faithful God; our realism from historical evidence and the deviance that resides in each of our hearts. Thus, our trust must be grounded in God and must be a gift that we request daily.

THEME 6: RESPONSIBILITY

THESIS: *Guided by Christian standards, we are to make moral decisions that are responsible and respectful of God's plan.*

> Does this progress, which has man for its author and promoter, make human life on earth "more human" in every aspect of that life? Does it make it more "worthy of man"? There can be no doubt that in various aspects it does. But the question keeps coming back with regard to what is most essential—whether in the context of this progress man, as man, is becoming truly better, that is to say more mature spiritually, more aware of the dignity of his humanity, more responsible, more open to others, especially the neediest and the weakest, and readier to give and to aid all. (15)

> The essential meaning of this "kingship" and "dominion" of man over the visible world, which the Creator himself gave man for his task, consists in the priority of ethics over technology, the primacy of the person over things, and in the superiority of spirit over matter. (16)

> The Declaration of Human Rights linked with the setting up of the United Nations organization certainly had its aim not only to depart from the horrible experiences of the last world war but also to create the basis for continual revision of programs, systems and regimes precisely from this single fundamental point of view, namely the welfare of man—or, let us say, of the person in the community—which must, as a fundamental factor in the common good, constitute the essential criterion for all programs, systems and regimes. (17)

Having laid the solid foundation of the mystery of redemption and the dignity of the human person, the encyclical moves to a point of great pragmatism. The living out of these basic truths demands the articulation of criteria and the call to specific responsibility. The criteria are clear: does a given action or product or movement enrich **the life of the** human person in community or not? Is the **person more** important than the thing; does morality give guidance to all forms of progress; is the common good carefully considered in the use of freedom? These are not abstract reflections from an ivory tower; rather, they are a concrete program for living life. Principles precede responsible behavior. The clearer these are, the more likelihood that they will be understood and put into practice.

Pope John Paul II is keenly aware that, as a matter of fact, the human person is often subordinated to lesser values. People are used as things *a la* the Playboy philosophy; individualism disregards the social dimension of life; materialism dominates over the spiritual dimensions of life; if something can be done it often is, whether or not it is ethically sound (test tube babies); people are discriminated against because of weakness or need. God's plan is that the dignity and worth of the human person be carefully safeguarded in all forms of behavior and attitudes. To deny man his dignity is to deny God proper respect; an offense to a daughter or son injures the father.

Progress, a proceeding forward, must be carefully measured. Where there is gain in one area of life there is often loss in another. The law of compensation is universal and irrevocable. The progress of technology can directly thwart the interior progress of the human person, though this is not inevitable. The Holy Father raises a profound question: "Do all the conquests attained until now and those projected for the future for technology accord with man's moral and spiritual progress?" (15) The temptations of acquisition are strong; the visibility of external achievement is very satisfying; the sense of power through control of the elements of nature can be overwhelming. The industrial and technological revolutions, with all of their blessings and benefits, must be evaluated also in terms of their effect on the spiritual and moral well-being of people. Perhaps the

time has come for that interior revolution by which we
assimilate and live out the basic principles of moral conduct;
the principle that love is the standard of all morality; that
justice applies to all relationships; that truthfulness sets us
free; that forgiveness and compassion heal and restore the
brokenness of life; that tolerance preserves our uniqueness
and principles safeguard our commonality; that leisure and
play are the right of every person; that discipline and sacrifice are essential to community living; that humor gives us
perspective and sustains a portion of our sanity; that God is
the power, wisdom and joy of our existence. If we progress
in incarnating such principles, true and authentic human
growth is present.

THEME 7: FREEDOM

THESIS: *The right to freedom is the cornerstone of human dignity
and a gift to be accepted and used with great respect.*

Today also, even after 2,000 years, we see Christ as the
one who brings man freedom based on truth, frees man
from what curtails, diminishes and as it were breaks off
this freedom at its root, in man's soul, his heart and his
conscience. What stupendous confirmation of this has
been given and is still given by those who, thanks to
Christ and in Christ, have reached true freedom and
have manifested it even in situations of external con-
straint! (12)

Nowadays it is sometimes held, though wrongfully, that
freedom is an end in itself, that each human being is free
when he makes use of freedom as he wishes, and that
this must be our aim in the lives of individuals and
societies. In reality, freedom is a great gift only when we
know how to use it consciously for everything that is our
true good. (21)

Since man's true freedom is not found in everything
that the various systems and individuals see and propa-
gate as freedom, the Church, because of her divine

mission, becomes all the more the guardian of this freedom, which is the condition and basis for the human person's true dignity. (12)

Like pesty gnats, though much more significant than these insects, ambiguity and ambivalence circle around the experience of freedom. Exactly what freedom is and how it is used is not clear; that freedom is needed to live a fully human life and yet can be most destructive causes mixed feelings. Whatever the price, we must seek clarity and struggle with a two-edged power. God has given us the gift and we must protect and promote it with courage and wisdom.

Freedom is blocked most clearly by slavery. Pope John Paul II admonishes us here: "Man cannot relinquish himself or the place in the visible world that belongs to him; he cannot become the slave of things, the slave of economic systems, the slave of production, the slave of his own products." (16) Abdication of freedom is probably the most practiced art in human history. Seeking to avoid responsibility, fearful of failure and rejection, unwilling to shoulder one's duty—these and countless other motives could be offered to explain the lack of moral growth within our lives. It is rather amusing, though sadly so, that in an age that apparently prizes freedom so highly, there are very few free persons. The weight of freedom, though not nearly proportionate to its joy, causes an initial fear that sends many into the slaveries of things, systems, production and products.

What is our true good? In what lies happiness? Until these questions are dealt with in an adequate way, freedom cannot be properly understood or exercised. Freedom is a means to an end. Its significance comes from this context. Once again we return to a serious problem of our century—the demise of metaphysics. Peter Berger, in his excellent work *A Rumor of Angels*, states: "The denial of metaphysics may here be identified with the triumph of triviality." (p. 94)

We might go even further: for want of a metaphysics there can be no triumph of anything, even triviality. Metaphysics fosters growth in our understanding of the true, the good, the beautiful. A Christian metaphysics sees in these aspects of being *the* Being, the end or goal of human existence. From this perspective freedom becomes meaningful and takes on its proper identity as a means, not idolized as an end that contains its own intrinsic significance.

What is most deeply human in our lives? We read: "In this creative restlessness beats and pulsates what is most deeply human—the search for truth, the insatiable need for the good, hunger for freedom, nostalgia for the beautiful, and the voice of conscience." (18) Among these pearls of humanness, shining brilliantly in our day, is the hunger for freedom. However, it is one of several important gems of human life. Surrounded by truth and goodness and conscience, it must respect these other fundamental elements and work with and through them in rich harmony. When one gem is respected and polished, all the others are thereby enriched; when one seeks predominance and exclusivity, the necklace becomes tarnished and blemished.

Freedom is a great and powerful gift—needing much care and love.

THEME 8: TRUTH

THESIS: *Truth, in its conception and expression, is a special responsibility of the Church and a primary means of contact with all people.*

> We perceive intimately that the truth revealed to us by God imposes on us an obligation. We have, in particular, a great sense of responsibility for this truth. By Christ's institution, the Church is its guardian and teacher, having been endowed with a unique assistance of the Holy Spirit in order to guard and teach it in its most exact integrity. (12)

. . . we have become sharers in this mission of the prophet Christ, and in virtue of that mission we together with him are serving divine truth in the Church. Being responsible for that truth also means loving it and seeking the most exact understanding of it, in order to bring it closer to ourselves and others in all its saving power, its splendor and its profundity joined with simplicity. (19)

As members of the people of God, they all have their own part to play in Christ's prophetic mission and service to divine truth, among other ways by an honest attitude toward truth, whatever field it may belong to, while educating others in truth and teaching them to mature in love and justice. Thus, a sense of responsibility for truth is one of the fundamental points of encounter between the Church and each man and also one of the fundamental demands determining man's vocation in the community of the Church. The present-day Church, guided by a sense of responsibility for truth, must persevere in fidelity to her own nature, which involves the prophetic mission that comes from Christ himself: "As the Father has sent me, even so I send you. . . . Receive the Holy Spirit." (19)

In an age that stresses relativity in epistemology and morality, the haunting refrain "what is truth?" can constantly be heard. Yet, just as there are scientific facts, there are also faith facts, and although the evidence for each varies, they remain facts nonetheless. The Church of Jesus Christ is mandated to communicate the truth that comes to her from scripture, tradition and experience. These invaluable sources provide us with contact with reality as well as a language system by which that experienced reality may be shared. While recognizing the limitations of any language system and its corresponding statements, the truth can be known and there is an obligation to transmit that truth as clearly and as simply as possible.

The encyclical implicitly stresses the importance of education and the significance of the institutions that carry on the work of communicating truth. The tone of the Holy Father's letter seems to hint that the obligation of promoting and guarding the truth is somewhat wanting. If this conjecture is correct, perhaps it flows from the emphasis in education on attitudes over content, process over product, values over action. Historically, this is to be expected—the pendulum swings. Previously we overemphasized content, product and action as a rather smug and narrow epistemological framework, oftentimes categorizing mysteries in rigid and static boxes. The pendulum has swung and we must once again consider what truths we are failing to give full weight to. Regardless, education is a key means by which the duty to share the truth can be fulfilled; our philosophy of education must therefore be clear and receive appropriate priority.

Truth is not a private affair. However brilliant an individual might be, his or her insights must be considered in a broader social context. A delicate balance here! Aquinas, Teilhard and many others have been questioned in questionable ways. The encyclical states: "Nobody, therefore, can make of theology as it were a simple collection of his own personal ideas, but everybody must be aware of being in close union with the mission of teaching truth for which the Church is responsible." (19) Our mission is the same as Jesus' vocation—to bring life, life to the full. By means of truth and freedom this is achieved.

An honest attitude toward truth underlies the Church's duty to maintain it. The Church must recognize truth wherever it emerges: in literature, in science, in economics, in politics, in technology. There need be no fear of the truth, though the truth is fearful. Just as the Church shares the truth of God and His love with the world, so too the Church must be open to receive the truth as it is articulated by competent philosophers, artists and believers across the world and history. The honest attitude toward truth is a two-way street; forgiveness for not practicing this attitude is also a two-way proposition.

THEME 9: UNITY

THESIS: *The call to unity (oneness) dominates the task of the Church and establishes a goal fulfilled only by love.*

The Church has only one life: that which is given her by her Spouse and Lord. Indeed, precisely because Christ united himself with her in his mystery of redemption, the Church must be strongly united with each man. (18)

The council document on non-Christian religions, in particular, is filled with deep esteem for the great spiritual values, indeed for the primacy of the spiritual, which in the life of mankind finds expression in religion and then in morality, with direct effect on the whole of culture. The Fathers of the Church rightly saw in the various religions as it were so many reflections of the one truth, "seeds of the word," attesting that, though the routes taken may be different, there is but a single goal to which is directed the deepest aspiration of the human spirit as expressed in its quest for God and also in its quest, through its tending toward God, for the full dimension of its humanity, or in other words for the full meaning of human life. (11)

The Church has always taught the duty to act for the common good, and, in so doing, has likewise educated good citizens for each state. Furthermore, she has always taught that the fundamental duty of power is solicitude for the common good of society; this is what gives power its fundamental rights. (17)

Deep within the recesses of our hearts we all know that we are made to be one with God, with others, indeed, one with ourselves. Unity brings peace; division causes endless restlessness. Jesus came to reconcile all creation back to the Father; as peacemaker he brings healing, his touch of love, to the alienations that separate us in every area of our life. To live in the awareness of God's oneness with us, his people, is to be holy. The covenant relationship fosters an intimacy beyond description and the Church is the mediator of this precious oneness.

Unity is threatened by many forces within ourselves and by powers that surround us in our environment. Our prejudices and hostilities cut us off from our brothers and sisters; greed and collective fears permeate the social air that we all breathe. Despite the factual trials and deep historical scarrings, we must have hope and strive with unmeasured energy to seek unity. Pope John Paul II writes: "We must therefore seek unity without being discouraged at the difficulties that can appear or accumulate along the road; otherwise we would be unfaithful to the word of Christ, we would fail to accomplish his testament." (6)

A renewed awareness of the common good is essential to oneness among peoples. With instant communication, the level of our social consciousness is being raised daily. What happens in one section of the planet is known to radically affect all others; our planet is a relatively small pond and the smallest stone has its rippled effects. Implicit in living out the common good is a high level of selflessness. This we cannot assume in ourselves nor in others. What is needed is love! Only when graced with the Spirit of Jesus' love will the world be capable of achieving the desired unity contained in our Father's plan.

Thus, we come back home to the center point of our Christianity: the Lord Jesus and the Eucharist. When Jesus dwells within us we live in a oneness which empowers us to bring about unity on our journey. By means of the Eucharist we come into vital contact with the Lord and are thus inspirited:

> It is an essential truth, not only of doctrine but also of life, that the Eucharist builds the Church, building it as the authentic community of the people of God, as the assembly of the faithful, bearing the same mark of unity that was shared by the apostles and the first disciples of the Lord. The Eucharist builds ever anew this community and unity, ever building and regenerating it on the basis of the sacrifice of Christ, since it commemorates his death on the cross, the price by which he redeemed us. (20)

When we become Eucharist to and for one another, then the dream will begin to take shape. But the price is high—we must be as bread that is broken. The cost of discipleship, indeed the cost of unity is the cross: a dying to self that others might live. Jesus has led the way and we are to follow, remembering that we go not only to, but through the cross into the land of resurrection, the land of oneness in which we experience peace and joy—love having been lived.

THEME 10: MISSION
THESIS: *The mission of the Church is the mission of Jesus: to reconcile, to serve, to love, to bring about peace.*

> Jesus Christ is the stable principle and fixed center of the mission that God himself entrusted to man. We must all share in this mission and concentrate all our forces on it, since it is more necessary than ever for modern mankind. (11)

> In this unity in mission, which is decided principally by Christ himself, all Christians must find what already united them, even before their full communion is achieved. This is apostolic and missionary unity, missionary and apostolic unity. Thanks to this unity we can together come close to the magnificent heritage of the human spirit that has been manifested in all religions, as

the Second Vatican Council's declaration *Nostra Aetate*
says. It also enables us to approach all cultures, all
ideological concepts, all people of good will. (12)

The aim of any service in the Church, whether the
service is apostolic, pastoral, priestly or episcopal, is to
keep up this dynamic link between the mystery of the
redemption and every man. (22)

Robert Frost, one snowy winter's eve, sat by the edge of a
woods that to him were "lovely, dark and deep." Though
wanting to linger and contemplate, there were promises
that he had to keep and he went off in answer to that call.
There is within Christianity an imperative of the same
nature—we are sent to all people and all nations to share the
message, more accurately to share the very person of Jesus,
who is the Word of our Father's love and forgiveness. Being
sent is as central to Christianity as breathing is to existence.

As a boomerang sails forth from the hand of the hunter,
returning only if it has missed its prey, the Christian
boomerang sails through history touching people with love
and causing an eternal remembrance of its sender. Jesus
came from the Father to redeem the world; that work must
continue. Indeed, how great is the harvest, as great as the
universe; how few are the missioned. The cause is not from a
lack of calling (vocation); rather, the respondents are well
below the predictable returns on any survey. And this is not
a matter of some doctoral dissertation.

The articulation of what the mission of the Church is
need not become unnecessarily complex. We are essentially
about one thing, and one thing alone:

The Church wishes to serve this single end: that each person
may be able to find Christ, in order that Christ may walk with
each person the path of life, with the power of the truth
about man and the world that is contained in the mystery of
the incarnation and the redemption and with the power of

the love that is radiated by that truth. Against a background of the ever increasing historical processes, which seem at the present time to have results especially within the spheres of various systems, ideological concepts of the world and regimes, Jesus Christ comes, in a way, newly present, in spite of all his apparent absences, in spite of all the limitations of the presence and of the institutional activity of the Church. Jesus Christ becomes present with the power of the love and truth that are expressed in him with unique unrepeatable fullness in spite of the shortness of his life on earth and the even greater shortness of his public activity. (13)

The Church's mission is extremely personal. It involves fellowship with Jesus Christ; a putting on of his mind and heart. Thus, St. Paul speaks of himself and other Christians as ambassadors of Christ, sent forth to carry his ideas, affections and words to others. What a noble task! What a splendid honor! What an awesome responsibility!

Certain individuals have a keen sense of mission. One whom I have personally known is a poet who articulated well the basic call of God. It is doubly fitting to conclude this chapter by quoting her poem because in it she uses Mary as the model of all Christians. Pope John Paul II also concluded *Redemptor Hominis* by giving special attention to Mary. Let us listen and respond with our hearts.

Into the hillside country Mary went
Carrying Christ, and all along the road
The Christ she carried generously bestowed
His grace on those she met. She had not meant
To tell she carried Christ. She was content
To hide His love for her. But about her glowed
Such joy that into stony hearts love flowed
And even to the unborn John Christ's grace was sent.

Christ in His Sacrament of love each day
Dwells in my soul a little space and then

I walk life's crowded highway, jostling men
Who seldom think of God. To these I pray
That I may carry Christ, for it may be
Some would not know of Him except through me.

                    (*Carrying Christ* by Ruth Mary Fox)

DIVES IN MISERICORDIA:
Themes and Theses

God's love and mercy are at the core of the Gospel message. In and through the life, death and resurrection of Jesus, these precious gifts are made visible. Divine love is so rich that, as it pierces the prism of human experience, it breaks forth in a grandeur that dazzles our imagination. God's love beating upon our stony hearts calls us to conversion; his love touching our sickness is the grace of healing; divine love enriching our emptiness means we are gifted as a people; the Father's love embracing the physical and moral threats and miseries of our lives is called mercy. Pope John Paul II, in his encyclical *Dives in Misericordia*, presents for our prayer, study and action the riches of God's faithful love and mercy. Fulfilling what he sees as his primary papal task, the implementation of the Second Vatican Council, the Holy Father describes at length the mystery of how God continues to restore broken humankind to its intrinsic value through the gift of mercy. The whole Church, and in a special way its ordained leaders, receives the mandates to reveal God's love for all persons in their individual and collective fragmentation and to beg God to continue to pour out his mercy upon their woundedness.

The purpose of this chapter is simple and modest: to select ten significant themes from the encyclical, to quote

passages from the encyclical that posit the theme and then to
give a short commentary expanding the theme. The choice
of each theme comes from its connection to the central
concept of mercy. This both limits and unifies our discussion. The reader is encouraged to study the original document in its entirety and only then to come to this essay for
further dialogue.

Pope John Paul II's first encyclical, *Redemptor Hominis*,
focuses on the dignity of the human person expressed
through the redemptive love of Christ. This present document draws our attention to the mystery of the Father and
his love, uniquely revealed through his mercy. It would not
be surprising if a future encyclical would deal with the role
of the Holy Spirit in the modern world focusing perhaps on
the concept of joy which constantly surfaces in many writings of the Holy Father.

THEME 1: JESUS
THESIS: *Jesus makes present the mercy and love of his Father by
means of his life, death and resurrection.*

> Making the Father present as love and mercy is, in
> Christ's own consciousness, the fundamental touch-
> stone of his mission as the Messiah. (3)

> The paschal mystery is the culmination of this revealing
> and effecting mercy, which is able to justify man, to
> restore justice in the sense of salvific order which God
> willed from the beginning in man and, through man, in
> the world. The suffering Christ speaks in a special way
> to man, and not only to the believer. The non-believer
> also will be able to discover in him the eloquence of
> solidarity with the human lot, as also the harmonious
> fullness of disinterested dedication to the cause of man,
> to truth and to love. (7)

> In fact, Christ, whom the Father "did not spare" for the
> sake of man and who in his passion and in the torment of
> the Cross did not obtain human mercy, has revealed in

his Resurrection the fullness of the love that the Father has for him and, in him, for all people. (8)

As a concept mercy seems uncomfortably abstract; as an experience, marvelously concrete. Once mercy is enfleshed in the words and deeds of an individual, it loses its ambiguity and abstractness. The elderly person hopelessly confused at an intersection is assisted by a passing stranger—we witness mercy in action. The motorist stranded in a winter's storm is aided by a fellow pilgrim—we witness mercy in action. The alienated child coming home after squandering health and love is graciously and joyfully embraced—we witness mercy in action. The life of Jesus Christ is a life of mercy made visible through his constant reaching out to those who were threatened interiorly by fear and darkness and exteriorly by misused freedom and corrupt power. The blind man can now see; the widow's son comes back to life; a loving gaze heals the betraying eyes of Peter; the gentle, firm words to the adulterous woman as he writes in the sand allows her accusers to leave without extravagant shame. In his embracing of the cross Jesus incarnates the mercy of the Father.

Individually and collectively we are challenged to put on the mind and heart of Jesus. In practical terms that means that we are first recipients of God's mercy when we become aware of the need within ourselves to be reconciled and forgiven. Breathing in that mercy, made accessible through Jesus, we then share it with others in our unique relationships and environments: caring for the powerless, humanizing our systems and institutions, lovingly confronting any form of enslavement that spells death to freedom. Jesus, living in us, continues the work of the Father. As willing instruments we cooperate with the flow of grace channeling God's mercy into the threatened corridors of human life. This noble vocation is a great privilege and an awesome responsibility.

THEME 2: MERCY

THESIS: *Mercy is God's love coming to console, heal and restore us when we are threatened or injured by physical and moral evil.*

> Especially through his life style and through his actions, Jesus revealed that love is present in the world in which we live—an effective love, a love that addresses itself to man and embraces everything that makes up his humanity. This love makes itself particularly noticed in contact with suffering, injustice and poverty—in contact with the whole historical "human condition," which in various ways manifests man's limitation and frailty, both physical and moral. (3)

> In the preaching of the prophets mercy signifies a special power of love, which prevails over the sin and infidelity of the chosen people. (4)

> Believing in the crucified Son means "seeing the Father," means believing that love is present in the world and that this love is more powerful than any kind of evil in which individuals, humanity, or the world are involved. Believing in this love means believing in mercy. For mercy is an indispensable dimension of love; it is as it were love's second name. (7)

Mercy is the graced response to definite historical realities with potential for great destruction; e.g. suffering, injustice, poverty, sin and infidelity. Instinctual drives make us either flee such traumatizing moments or strike out in self-protecting vengeance. Jesus lived our history; he embraced our condition; he responded in love. Love in the face of these potentially destructive life-experiences is called mercy.

Love need not be effective. If the intended loving act or word does not touch the experience of the other or if the lover lives apart from the circumstances of those loved, then love fails to achieve its intended effect—the giving of life.

The encyclical states that Jesus was someone gifted with compassionate insight allowing him to touch people in the uniqueness of their situation, someone who experienced solidarity with people by embracing their circumstances. Such authenticity compels belief. Because Jesus walked our road and tasted our pain, because he lived our poverty and was subject to our injustice, because he was the victim of sin and infidelity, authority flowed from his every word and deed. He experienced life from the inside; he was no stranger to the paradoxes and enigmas of human existence. Yet despite the hurt and agony, Jesus continued to love and to reveal the Father's mercy. Knowing well how different our response has been in many instances, this mercy of God boggles our imagination and challenges our very lives.

Love is a form of power for it effects change. It is but one form of power that has an impact on the lives of people. Power is easily distorted because of the complexity of motivation, the subtle machinations of our feelings, the sheer thrill of exercising control. Graced power is the use of an energy that respects all individuals affected. In the face of injury and harm there is an almost automatic drive to preserve self regardless of the means. Such a response can easily be destructive. Gifted with mercy, a person need not respond to threats and attacks in violent ways. Mercy restores nobility: in the face of being victimized one continues to love and refuses to be drawn into the trap of becoming a victimizer in turn.

THEME 3: DIGNITY

THESIS: *Human dignity, lost by sin and oppression, is restored by divine mercy.*

> Man cannot be manifested in the full dignity of his nature without reference—not only on the level of concepts but also in an integrally existential way—to God.

Man and man's lofty calling are revealed in Christ through the revelation of the mystery of the Father and his love. (1)

The truth, revealed in Christ, about God the "Father of mercies," enables us to "see" him as particularly close to man, especially when man is suffering, when he is under threat at the very heart of his existence and dignity. And this is why, in the situation of the Church and the world today, many individuals and groups guided by a lively sense of faith are turning, I would say almost spontaneously, to the mercy of God. (2)

The inheritance that the [prodigal] son had received from his father was a quantity of material goods, but more important than these goods was his dignity as a son in his father's house. The situation in which he found himself when he lost the material goods should have made him aware of the loss of that dignity ... the tragedy of lost dignity, the awareness of squandered sonship. (5)

In analyzing the parable of the prodigal son, we have already called attention to the fact that he who forgives and he who is forgiven encounter one another at an essential point, namely the dignity or essential value of the person, a point which cannot be lost and the affirmation of which, or its rediscovery, is a source of the greatest joy. (14)

A current expression used in many walks of life is "bottom line"; when all is said and done, what is it that really counts? The bottom line value in human existence is dignity: a sense of self-worth and self-respect. Take away this keystone and the structure of one's personality crumbles. Suicide is not an infrequent response to the absence of dignity. Other less drastic but destructive responses are drug addiction, alcoholism, misuse of power and affluence, distorted forms of sexuality. Lost dignity cannot look in the mirror.

The mystery of God's love and mercy restores the dignity lost through sin and exploitation. The bottom line is that God loves us so faithfully that no infidelity nor frantic flight can prevent our escape from his gentle embrace. Our dignity is grounded in divine concern; it is anchored in a relationship of Creator-creature, Lover-beloved. Radical faith is essential at this point. We come to believe that our very identity rests in creaturehood and in the fact that we have a common Father. Jesus came that these truths might enlighten our minds and enflame our hearts. By embracing our condition, Jesus brought us freedom and truth enabling us to experience our incredible dignity and worth in his sight. St. Catherine of Siena powerfully experienced this dignity:

> O mad lover! And you have need of your creature? It seems so to me, for you act as if you could not live without her, in spite of the fact that you are Life itself, and everything has life from you and nothing can have life without you. Why then are you so mad? Because you have fallen in love with what you have made![1]

Therein resides our dignity: we are loved.

This dignity needs nurturing and protecting. It can be squandered in a variety of ways: opting for material goods over God's dominion—idolatry; desiring control over surrender—Eden revisited; longing for satiation by fleeing poverty—avarice. Dignity is not a static reality. It must be fostered by careful tending. Prayer sustains a vision of what that dignity is. Simplicity helps us avoid confusing dignity's essential role from all that is accidental. Discernment enables us to make choices congruent with our authentic identity. All this is possible because of Jesus, the one who empowers us through his Spirit to embrace our weakness and therein find our dignity.

THEME 4: CONVERSION

THESIS: *Conversion provides evidence that mercy is active in our world.*

> The parable of the prodigal son expresses in a simple but profound way the reality of conversion. Conversion is the most concrete expression of the working of love and of the presence of mercy in the human world. (6)
>
> Conversion to God always consists in discovering his mercy, that is, in discovering that love which is patient and kind as only the Creator and Father can be; the love to which the "God and Father of our Lord Jesus Christ" is faithful to the uttermost consequences in the history of his covenant with man; even to the Cross and to the death and resurrection of the Son. Conversion to God is always the fruit of the "rediscovery" of his Father, who is rich in mercy. (13)
>
> Authentic knowledge of the God of mercy, the God of tender love, is a constant and inexhaustible source of conversion, not only as a momentary interior act but also as a permanent attitude, as a state of mind. Those who come to know God in this way, who "see" him in this way, can live only in a state of being continually converted to him. They live, therefore, *in statu conversionis*; and it is this state of conversion which marks out the most profound element of the pilgrimage of every man and woman on earth *in statu viatoris*. (13)

Saul's journey to Damascus is filled with drama. Persecuting the Christian community with fanatical zeal, this powerful man was unexpectedly thrown into the stream of God's marvelous grace. Years later he writes to the people of Rome of his constant struggle to live out the life of grace (Rm 7). This apostle to the Gentiles was not "converted." Rather he entered a process of conversion that was lifelong. How did this process begin, continue and seek completion? In Christ Jesus, the mercy of the Father's love made visible!

God is after our minds and hearts, our memories and imaginations. Conversion takes place at these deep regions. Mercy creeps in through the cracks and crevices, stirring the conscience, inspiring an image, provoking a thought, sweeping the heart of debris. Divine mercy touches what is unredeemed and heals wounds that fester from years of neglect. With infinite respect and exquisite timing, God turns our mind back to Truth, our heart to Love, our memory to the Promise, our imagination to Hope.

Moving from darkness to light is a lifelong process. Given the human condition, conversion is seen as a permanent disposition demanding of us constant surrender and dying to self. The paschal mystery calls us to participate ever more deeply in this experience we call life. Like a spiral we turn from darkness to light and in that light we discover new and deeper darknesses from which we must now turn. The temptation is to want to plateau, to reach a certain point of growth and then level off. Temporary oases are fine but after an hour or two we must be back on the road. Pushed by the Father's initiative and drawn by the risen Lord's love we continue our journey in joy.

Mercy, like any virtue, is subject to the incarnational principle. Its full reality is seen in its expression. The historical fact of conversion documents that mercy has been and is being enfleshed. We need not focus simply on great sinners who became saints through grace. We need but look into our own hearts and communities to see how Jesus has mercifully drawn us into the posture of receiving and then shared his forgiveness. Thus the miser in us becomes generous and poor; our arrogant observations are overwhelmed by incomprehensible mystery; our apathy, through grace, is launched into supreme activity. How rich is God in his mercy! How marvelous is his work of conversion in our lives!

THEME 5: JOY
THESIS: *God's merciful love overflows into joy.*

The father of the prodigal son is faithful to his fatherhood, faithful to the love that he had always lavished on
his son. This fidelity is expressed in the parable not only
by his immediate readiness to welcome him home when
he returns after having squandered his inheritance; it is
expressed even more fully by that joy, that merrymaking for the squanderer after his return, merrymaking
which is so generous that it provokes the opposition and
hatred of the elder brother, who had never gone far
away from his father and had never abandoned the
home. (6)

In the same Chapter 15 of Luke's Gospel, we read the
parable of the sheep that was found and then the parable of the coin that was found. Each time there is an
emphasis on the same joy that is present in the case of
the prodigal son. The father's fidelity to himself is totally
concentrated upon the humanity of the lost son, upon
his dignity. This explains above all his joyous emotion at
the moment of the son's return home. (6)

The father first and foremost expresses to him his joy
that he has been "found again" and that he has "re-
turned to life." This joy indicates a good that has remained intact; even if he is a prodigal, a son does not
cease to be truly his father's son; it also indicates a good
that has been found again, which in the case of the
prodigal son was his return to the truth about himself.
(6)

Mercy confronts a most serious and "heavy" aspect of
life: misplaced value, sin, injury, hurt, violence. An important question arises: in what manner will divine mercy be
expressed, given the distasteful object it must embrace? If
that expression be in any way demeaning or humiliating,
mercy may well be shunned rather than sought. Scripture
reveals Jesus showing us how the Father's mercy is to be

manifest: the mercy-giver, God the Father, is filled with joy and merrymaking. Again the good news is almost too good to be true.

Simone Weil has written:

> We know that joy is the sweetness of contact with the love of God, that affliction is the wound of this same contact when it is painful, and that only the contact matters, not the manner of it.[2]

Here we discern a clue to the mystery of joy residing in mercy: joy is consequent upon the awareness of God's presence and encounter regardless of whether we are in sin or grace. If in grace, we experience his presence as loving union; if in sin, we experience his presence as love in the form of mercy. Despondency, that haunting specter that stifles joy, captures our existence when we fail to realize that mercy is available to our sinful condition. In our discouragement we focus on the separation that our sin causes and neglect to search out God's love and forgiveness. We are afraid to face his gaze and yet, in a paradox that baffles our imagination, that painful risk is necessary to experience the joy stemming from an encounter with infinite mercy. Francis Thompson said it well when he called God "this tremendous lover."

Is our God one of supreme joy? Is our God one of merry-making? An affirmative answer demands that in spite of so much sin throughout the world there must be a vision of something glorious and good. What did Jesus see that allowed him to tell the story of a prodigal father who insists, against strong family opposition, that a joyous banquet must be celebrated upon his son's return? What did Jesus experience in the depth of his heart when, though sin was in the air at the last supper, he shared his joy-filled discourse with his disciples? A vision of love! Sin meets mercy and joy results. Only a vision of such depth allows for joy in the face of physical and moral evil. Dignity is regained, the wound healed, paradise restored! The human person opening up to God's embrace fills creation with alleluias and it's Easter once again.

THEME 6: LOVE

THESIS: *Love is mercy writ large, overpowering sin and death, and revealing the fidelity of the Father in Jesus.*

It is significant that in their preaching the prophets link mercy, which they often refer to because of the people's sins, with the incisive image of love on God's part. The Lord loves Israel with the love of a special choosing, much like the love of a spouse, and for this reason he pardons its sins and even its infidelities and betrayals. (4)

Here is the Son of God, who in his Resurrection experienced in a radical way mercy shown to himself, that is to say the love of the Father which is more powerful than death. And it is also the same Christ, the Son of God, who at the end of his messianic mission—and, in a certain sense, even beyond the end—reveals himself as the inexhaustible source of mercy, of the same love that, in a subsequent perspective of the history of salvation in the Church, is to be everlastingly confirmed as more powerful than sin. The paschal Christ is the definitive incarnation of mercy, its living sign: in salvation history and in eschatology. (8)

With this cry let us, like the sacred writers, call upon the God who cannot despise anything that he has made, the God who is faithful to himself, to his Fatherhood and his love. And, like the prophets, let us appeal to that love which has maternal characteristics and which, like a mother, follows each of her children, each lost sheep, even if they should number millions, even if in the world evil should prevail over goodness, even if contemporary humanity should deserve a new "flood" on account of its sins, as once the generation of Noah did. Let us have recourse to that fatherly love revealed to us by Christ in his messianic mission, a love which reached its culmination in his cross, in his death and resurrection. (15)

In his excellent study *The Prophetic Imagination*, Walter Brueggemann states that the function of the prophet is to criticize and to energize. By means of these activities, the community is challenged to be faithful to its deepest values and to be filled with hope in God's promise. Key to the prophetic task is to constantly remind the people of God's love as manifest in his fidelity:

> But a prophet has another purpose in bringing hope to public expression, and that is to return the community to its single referent, the sovereign faithfulness of God.[3]

God's loving mercy deals with our infidelities and betrayals, our spiritual prostitutions and exploited friendships. The power of sin defies description: anguish rending the human heart; anxieties making us friends of insomnia; guilt badgering our nerves without surcease; self-disgust paralyzing our will. What can possibly break the power of sin that is so destructive? Revelation draws us to accept the mystery of God's love which overpowers sin. That love is then to condition our lives so that we might make it present in our words and deeds. Faith allows us to experience this love and to enter into the process of making it real for others.

Death, no less than sin, must kneel before divine mercy. Herein we find a love that is stronger than death. Death's power seems so total that all existence trembles before its inevitability. All creation has been made subject to the dying process. Yet, in Jesus, who is the love of the Father, all creation will one day be made new. The mystery of love is seen in the cross. Indeed the cross tells of sin and death, caused by our misguided freedom; it also proclaims how extravagant is God's love for us. Death has lost its finality because of Good Friday; the ultimate sting is gone. Through the grace of mercy, God's love makes possible hope, a hope that both sin and death attempt to extinguish. Thus we come to realize that in the crucified Lord the fidelity and love of God is enfleshed. Johannes Metz describes it this way:

> God's fidelity to man is what gives man the courage to be true to himself. And the legacy of this total commitment to mankind, the proof of his fidelity to our poverty, is the cross. The cross is the sacrament of poverty of spirit, the sacrament of authentic humanness in a sinful world. It is the sign that one remained true to his humanity, that he accepted it in full obedience.[4]

THEME 7: JUSTICE

THESIS: *Justice must be supplemented by mercy if it is to avoid distortion and narrow expression.*

> The Church shares with the people of our time this profound and ardent desire for a life which is just in every aspect, nor does she fail to examine the various aspects of the sort of justice that the life of people and society demands. This is confirmed by the field of Catholic social doctrine, greatly developed in the course of the last century. On the lines of this teaching proceed the education and formation of human consciences in the spirit of justice, and also individual undertakings, especially in the sphere of the apostolate of the laity, which are developing in precisely this spirit. (12)

> And yet, it would be difficult not to notice that very often programs which start from the idea of justice and which ought to assist its fulfillment among individuals, groups and human societies, in practice suffer from distortions. Although they continue to appeal to the ideal of justice, nevertheless experience shows that other negative forces have gained the hand over justice, such as spite, hatred and even cruelty. In such cases, the desire to

annihilate the enemy, limit his freedom, or even force him into total dependence, becomes the fundamental motive for action; and this contrasts with the essence of justice, which by its very nature tends to establish equality and harmony between parties in conflict. (12)

Thus, mercy becomes an indispensable element for shaping mutual relationships between people in a spirit of deepest respect for what is human and in a spirit of mutual brotherhood. It is impossible to establish this bond between people if they wish to regulate their mutual relationships solely according to the measure of justice. In every sphere of interpersonal relationships justice must, so to speak, be "corrected" to a considerable extent by that love which, as St. Paul proclaims, "is patient and kind" or, in other words, possesses the characteristics of that merciful love which is so much of the essence of the Gospel and Christianity. (14)

The relationship between mercy-love and justice needs careful reflection. The Gospel is concerned with human beings who have rights and duties. The good news is also concerned with attitudes and actions that go far beyond giving all people their due. Love, not justice, is the core of Jesus' teaching. However, because justice too often is neglected in the name of charity, both levels of human interaction must be protected and promoted.

Justice is an extremely rich concept. On the individual level justice deals with natural and acquired rights as well as absolute and conditional obligations. Social justice calls for a keen sensitivity to patterns of behavior that foster peace among groupings of people. As nations continue to grow close to each other, international justice becomes a matter of urgent concern. In all of these areas a basic principle applies: there is no peace without justice and there is no justice without a deep concern and reverence for the common good.

History records volumes of injustices in every segment

of society. We realize that the context for seeking peace that is based on justice is in a fragile, fragmented world. We risk hurts and severe injury when we attempt to respond to the call of justice. The encyclical serves us well in stating that because of the human condition justice alone is not sufficient because it can be permeated so easily with spite, hatred and cruelty. Thus justice must be seen as more than a series of programs and activities; its authentic heartbeat must be founded on mutual respect and a profound desire for harmony.

Only a justice enriched by merciful love can promote the type of human community called for by Jesus. While never backing off from the demands of an objective justice, compassion must be its wellspring. Left to ourselves and basic instinctual tendencies for revenge, there is a sense of helplessness in becoming just persons. God's grace is needed if we are to live in peace founded on justice. Given the volatile world situation, the urgency of the matter leads us to a deep prayer that the Spirit of justice and merciful love transform our personal lives, our systems and our institutions.

THEME 8: FORGIVENESS

THESIS: *Forgiveness is God's merciful love that overpowers sin while demanding that the requirements of justice be sustained.*

> Mercy in itself, as a perfection of the infinite God, is also infinite. Also infinite therefore and inexhaustible is the Father's readiness to receive the prodigal children who return to his home. Infinite are the readiness and power of forgiveness which flow continually from the marvelous value of the sacrifice of the Son. (13)

> Society can become "ever more human" only when we introduce into all the mutual relationships which form its moral aspect the moment of forgiveness, which is so much of the essence of the Gospel. Forgiveness demon-

strates the presence in the world of the love which is more powerful than sin. Forgiveness is also the fundamental condition for reconciliation, not only in the relationship of God with man, but also in relationships between people. (14)

Christ emphasizes so insistently the need to forgive others that when Peter asked him how many times he should forgive his neighbor he answered with the symbolic number of "seventy times seven," meaning that he must be able to forgive everyone every time. It is obvious that such a generous requirement of forgiveness does not cancel out the objective requirements of justice. Properly understood, justice constitutes, so to speak, the goal of forgiveness. In no passage of the Gospel message does forgiveness, or mercy as its source, mean indulgence towards evil, towards scandals, towards injury or insult. In any case, reparation for evil and scandal, compensation for injury, and satisfaction for insult are conditions for forgiveness. (14)

When asked how they are to pray, Jesus taught the disciples a prayer that embraced every dimension of life: spiritually, we are to focus on the Father and his will; physically, we are to turn to the Father in trusting faith to ask for our daily bread; personally and socially, we are mandated to have forgiving, compassionate love. The Lord's prayer implicitly reveals a God who is always ready to forgive. Made to his image and likeness, we are challenged to follow that divine mercy by imitating God's healing love. The gift of the Spirit makes possible this response.

Ordinary People, an award-winning motion picture, presented in dramatic form a family torn apart by tragedy, mental illness and a breakdown in communication. A lack of forgiveness prevented reconciliation. In the story a mother had lost her favorite son in a boating accident. She was unable to forgive her younger son who was sailing with the older brother when the accident occurred. Eventually this lack of forgiveness led to a split in the family. Jesus came to reconcile; he came to mend what had been torn; he yearned that all people be one. The basis for this unity is the grace of forgiveness. Conscious of our own sins and that we have received forgiveness from God, we must now share that gift with others in a manner similar to the way in which the Lord healed us.

Forgiveness is not a whitewash! Central to forgiveness is the realization of justice. This calls for reciprocity and mutuality in the reconciliation process. Both the victim and the victimizer must be of such a disposition that harmony can result and justice be done. Revenge and spite on the part of the injured person blockş the process; want of proper physical and moral satisfaction on the part of the victimizer precludes true reconciliation. Although God's love is unconditional and we are challenged to emulate this charity, neither love nor forgiveness can be forced or realized unless all parties are authentically disposed.

THEME 9: VALUES

THESIS: *Values that are injured or lost are restored when mercy is exercised in the community.*

> Mercy—as Christ has presented it in the parable of the prodigal son—has the interior form of the love that in the New Testament is called *agape*. This love is able to reach down to every prodigal son, to every human misery, and above all to every form of moral misery, to sin. When this happens, the person who is the object of mercy does not feel humiliated, but rather found again and "restored to value." (6)

> The true and proper meaning of mercy does not consist only in looking, however penetratingly and compassionately, at moral, physical or material evil: mercy is manifested in its true and proper aspect when it restores to value, promotes and draws good from all the forms of evil existing in the world and in man. (6)

The Church, having before her eyes the picture of the generation to which we belong, shares the uneasiness of so many of the people of our time. Moreover, one cannot fail to be worried by the decline of many fundamental values, which constitute an unquestionable good not only for Christian morality but simply for human morality, for moral culture. These values include respect for human life from the moment of conception, respect for marriage in its indissoluble unity, and respect for the stability of the family. Moral permissiveness strikes especially at this most sensitive sphere of life and society. Hand in hand with this go the crisis of truth in human relationships, lack of responsibility for what one says, the purely utilitarian relationship between individual and individual, the loss of a sense of the authentic common good and the ease with which this good is alienated. Finally, there is the "desacralization" that often turns into "dehumanization": the individual and the society for whom nothing is "sacred" suffer moral decay, in spite of appearances. (12)

As stated earlier in this chapter, human dignity is the keystone supporting the fullness of life. Yet a galaxy of other values surround human dignity and these values, like dignity, are the object of attack in a culture enmeshed in materialism, consumerism and superficiality. Truth is threatened by myopia and prejudices; human life fails to find due respect supposedly because of economic stress and personal inconvenience; marriage and its unity is torpedoed by poor modeling and failure in communication; rugged individualism still defies the call to human solidarity and the common good; the good earth fails to find a friend in the human community; the powerless and weak are easily discarded because they lack competence and do not contribute to the GNP. Jesus came to bring life, life that is blessed if based on deep values: poverty of spirit, gentleness, compassion, mercy, purity, peace, justice. He not only taught these values. He lived them in a unique way and by his example showed that values must be much more than just notional concepts residing in our minds; they must reside in our hearts and overflow into word and deed.

Mercy is the divine technology that enables us to rebuild an authentic community precisely at that moment when our central values are threatened. In the face of a lie, we firmly search for and articulate the truth; when confronted with violence, mercy empowers us to refrain from striking back. As cold silence invades our homes and hearts, mercy enkindles in us the desire for dialogue. Presented with the option of narrow parochialism, we beg for the merciful grace to break forth from our small worlds and embrace all people as members of our family. When tempted to greed, to power, to competition, mercy empowers us to put down our weapons and reach for instruments of peace.

Values are deep realities. From them spring our decisions and life styles. Jesus addressed people at the depth level, at the heart of our value system. This is the area where sin is also operative. Indeed, touch a person's values and you have reached the core of human life. Personal and communal sin verifies that our value system has been invaded and damaged; the coming of Jesus and his redemptive activity attests to a marvellous restoration. Creation is stupendous, even more so God's recreative work of redemption. Mercy restores our values and makes us fully human and capable of divine life.

THEME 10: MISSION

THESIS: *Mercy is an integral part of the Church's mission; the task being to reveal God and his merciful love to all.*

Christ's messianic program, the program of mercy, becomes the program of his people, the program of the Church. At its very center there is always the cross, for it is in the cross that the revelation of merciful love attains its culmination. Until "the former things pass away," the cross will remain the point of reference. . . (8)

The Church must bear witness to the mercy of God revealed in Christ, in the whole of his mission as Messiah, professing it in the first place as a salvific truth of faith and as necessary for a life in harmony with faith, and then seeking to introduce it and to make it incarnate in the lives both of her faithful and as far as possible in the lives of all people of good will. Finally, the Church—professing mercy and remaining always faithful to it—has the right and the duty to call upon the mercy of God, imploring it in the face of all the manifestations of physical and moral evil, before all the threats that cloud the whole horizon of the life of humanity today. (13)

In continuing the great task of implementing the Second Vatican Council, in which we can rightly see a new phase of the self-realization of the Church—in keeping with the epoch in which it has been our destiny to live—the Church herself must be constantly guided by the full consciousness that in this work it is not permissible for her, for any reason, to withdraw into herself. The reason for her existence is, in fact, to reveal God, that Father who allows us to "see" him in Christ. No matter how strong the resistance of human history may be, no matter how marked the diversity of contemporary civilization, no matter how great the denial of God in the human world, so much the greater must be the Church's closeness to that mystery which, hidden for centuries in God, was then truly shared with man, in time, through Jesus Christ. (15)

The Church must constantly be in touch with her identity and mission. As a community of believers in Jesus and as a people committed to build up the kingdom that he professed, we come to know ourselves as sent, sent to announce the good news of the Father's merciful love. As the heart of its mission, the Church rejoices in the riches of God's mercy. This vocation can be seen in the various models of the Church:[5] (1) as *the people of God* the Church is born out of God's love and mercy; (2) as a *sacrament*, the Church makes present in visible, tangible ways the miracle of forgiveness; (3) as an *institution* the Church organizes and administers the gifts of the people so that all creation might encounter the divine touch of healing; (4) as *herald* the Church never ceases to shout out from the mountain and housetop the message of the Father's compassion; and (5) as *servant* the Church humbly asks for mercy for herself and then generously shares it with all peoples. Whatever model we use we see the importance and centrality of mercy to her mission.

Mercy is a gift from God. It is sheer grace. In personal and communal prayer we humbly turn to God begging him that this precious gift might be effected in us and in his entire world. Our mission and ministry is grounded in this prayerful stance; we well know that all life, all holiness and all mercy comes from our Father. Indeed, our receptivity to divine mercy will be proportionate to the quality of our prayer life.

The hungers of the human heart are many. One of the deepest desires is the knowledge and assurance that our relationship with God is whole. This felt knowledge we call peace; this peace is possible because of divine forgiveness flowing from mercy. The mission of the Church is to help people see the mystery of God and to foster unity between God and his people. That mission is threatened by the blindness of rationalism, the angst of existentialism, the ultimate meaninglessness of positivism. These movements must not deter the Church from fostering the vision that Jesus has given us nor from bringing about the unity that he so deeply longed for. This task is accomplished most effectively when God's love and mercy can be found and seen in the eyes and hearts of his people. What a noble mission; what an honored privilege.

Footnotes

1. Catherine of Siena, *The Dialogue*, trans. by Suzanne Noffke, O.P. (New York: Paulist Press, 1980), 325.
2. *The Simone Weil Reader*, ed. George A. Panichas (New York: David McKay Company, Inc., 1977), 107.
3. Walter Brueggemann, *The Prophetic Imagination* (Philadelphia: Fortress Press, 1978), 68.
4. Johannes Baptist Metz, *Poverty of Spirit*, trans. by John Drury (New York: Paulist Press, 1968), 19.
5. Avery Dulles, *Models of the Church* (New York: Image Books, 1974).

LABOREM EXERCENS:
Themes and Theses

Several years ago Studs Terkel published a series of masterfully conducted interviews under the title of *Working*. People from various fields of life reflected candidly on the meaning or lack of meaning that work had in their lives. What fascinates the reader is the blatant honesty of those interviewed; they told it the way they experienced it. With deep feeling and perceptive observation, these working people revealed the movements of their mind and heart.

On September 14, 1981, Pope John Paul II shared his third encyclical letter, *Laborem Exercens*, with the world. This papal document focuses on the topic of work, that human activity at once so universally experienced and yet so frequently devoid of meaning. What Terkel did on the experiential level, the Holy Father does on the reflective level. We do not find personal interviews with the rank and file but, from a scriptural and faith point of view, a description of the theological underpinning of our obligation to work. Within this perspective he discusses many questions: the nature and meaning of work; the relationship of work to the person, family and society; how work is influenced by various ideologies; the duty and rights of the worker; a spirituality of work. Rather than delineate detailed and specific policies, the encyclical is concerned with articulating certain principles and guidelines to govern the formation of policy for specific situations. When these principles are adequately and properly applied, work helps to build up the world community and becomes a means of safeguarding the humanity of all.

These reflections of the Holy Father are extremely relevant. In an age when technology can so easily control the course of history we must hear over and over again the principle that people have primacy over things. In a period of history that takes for granted exploitation and manipulation as acceptable life styles, we must have confirmation that persons are ends and not means. In our rapidly moving century that gives low priority to quiet and reflective times, it is healthy to have our attention drawn to an awareness of the importance of rest within the spirituality of work. Written on the ninetieth anniversary of Leo XIII's *Rerum Novarum*, this present encyclical continues to remind us of the importance of these social questions and the function that the Church plays in their solution in public life.

THEME 1: THE MEANING AND DIGNITY OF WORK

THESIS: *Work is an active process by which creative and productive persons gain dominion over the earth and achieve fullness as human beings.*

> Understood as a process whereby man and the human race subdue the earth, work corresponds to this basic biblical concept only when throughout the process man manifests himself and confirms himself as the one who "dominates." (6)

> Work is a good thing for man—a good thing for his humanity—because throughout work man not only transforms nature, adapting it to his own needs, but he also achieves fulfillment as a human being and indeed, in a sense, becomes "more a human being." (9)

> Man must work, both because the Creator has commanded it and because of his own humanity, which

requires work in order to be maintained and developed. Man must work out of regard for others, especially his own family, but also for the society he belongs to, the country of which he is a member, since he is the heir to the work of generations and at the same time a sharer in building the future of those who will come after him in the succession of history. (16)

The farmer gazes out on newly acquired property and perceives the rocks, tree stumps and weeds; a year later that same farmer, after much labor, rejoices in an autumn harvest of grain. The artist sits before a small mound of clay; many hours later a finely crafted vessel receives the accolades of admiring friends. The steel worker feeds the furnace knowing that when the final product is completed, beams of steel will be available for buildings and bridges. The human person, taking the many resources of the world, fashions them into useful and beautiful objects in the meeting of human needs. This process, both creative and productive, brings order out of chaos. The newly won unity fills the human spirit with a sense of meaning, peace and joy.

A radical call to all of us is the call to become human persons. Within that universal vocation work plays a necessary and significant part. Only when we thoughtfully expend the energy given to us do we develop our potential and actualize our gifts. Work and growth demand that we participate in this venture of becoming human. Gifts unemployed atrophy. Needs unmet cause suffering. Lack of human development means boredom and despair. Emerson knew the value of work and its effect on human growth:

> I hear therefore with joy whatever is beginning to be said of the dignity and necessity of labor to every citizen. There is virtue yet in the hoe and the spade, for learned as well as for the unlearned hands.[1]

This labor must be balanced and rational, respecting

individuals and allowing for personal fulfillment. History provides evidence that when certain forms of work do not have these qualities human beings are dehumanized and even destroyed.

In his perceptive and challenging philosophical treatise, *Leisure, the Basis of Culture*, the neo-Thomist Josef Pieper describes "workism" as an attitude and ideology that disregards the essential nature of work. Pieper's argument is that work is meaningful only when the human person's dignity is fully appreciated and when the activity of work is complemented by a certain receptivity towards life which is called contemplation. The present encyclical also protects this balance and perspective.

THEME 2: THE SUBJECTIVE AND OBJECTIVE DIMENSIONS OF WORK

THESIS: *The subjective dimension of work (the dignity of the human person) always has priority over the objective dimension (productivity).*

The very process of "subduing the earth," that is to say work, is marked in the course of history, and especially in recent centuries, by an immense development of technological means. This is an advantageous and positive phenomenon, on condition that the objective dimension of work does not gain the upper hand over the subjective dimension, depriving man of his dignity and inalienable rights or reducing them. (10)

... man's dominion over the earth is achieved in and by means of work. There thus emerges the meaning of work in an objective sense, which finds expression in the various epochs of culture and civilization. Man dominates the earth by the very fact of domesticating animals, rearing them and obtaining from them the food and clothing he needs, and by the fact of being able to extract various natural resources from the earth and the seas. (5)

> As a person, man is therefore the subject of work. As a
> person he works, he performs various actions belonging
> to the work process; independently of their objective
> content, these actions must all serve to realize his hu-
> manity, to fulfill the calling to be a person that is his by
> reason of his very humanity. (6)

Work always involves a person, a process and a product.
The language of the encyclical refers to the person as the
subject of work (the subjective dimension) while the product
is the object of work (the objective dimension). This distinction is important: a product does not have interiority, nor is
it a center of thought and love, nor is it destined for immor-
tality. On the other hand, the human person is spiritual,
immortal and called to fullness of life in God. The process of
work can take such a direction so as to make a person play
the role of a mere tool (cog in the machine). The focus is on
productivity. Such a procedure used in the work world
dehumanizes the person and negates the Christian meaning
of work. Unfortunately, history records too many years of
such abuse.

The Holy Father's analysis of work contains an implicit
anthropology, one that has the highest regard for the fullness of human life. Every person has both an inner and
outer agenda. Meister Eckhart describes it this way:

> There are people who squander the strength of their souls in
> the outward man. These are the people, all of whose desires
> and thoughts turn on transient goods, since they are una-
> ware of the inner person. Sometimes a good man robs his
> outward person of all the soul's agents, in order to dispatch
> them on some higher enterprise; so, conversely animal
> people rob the inner person of the soul's agents and assign
> them to the outward man. A man may be ever so active
> outwardly and still leave the inner man unmoved and
> passive.[2]

Both the outer and inner dimensions of work need protection and a sensitive balance. Each has its own unique value. If they are not integrated, a person either "sells his soul to the company store" or falls into a type of narcissism which destroys communal responsibility. Persons have dignity which must not be denied; the work process must be respected as part of God's plan; human life is impossible without those products which meet essential needs.

Proper priority and balance in reference to the subjective and objective dimensions of work are maintained when *reverence* is present among people. Only when we stand in awe of every person, only when we hold sacred the gifts of air, water and land, only when we carefully consider the inner dynamism and value of the creative process will we truly appreciate work. Goethe reminds us: "The shudder of awe is humanity's highest faculty." This papal document contains that "shudder of awe." Whenever we encounter the handiwork of God, human or otherwise, we bow before the Creator's reflection. The person, the *imago Dei*, the creative process and end product of our work demand appropriate respect.

THEME 3: THE VALUE SCALE OF WORK
THESIS: *Work involves three spheres of values: (1) a personal value bringing dignity to the individual; (2) a family value forming the foundation of communal life; and (3) a societal value enriching the common good.*

> It [work] is not only good in the sense that it is useful or something to enjoy; it is also good as being something worthy, that is to say, something that corresponds to man's dignity, that expresses this dignity and increases it. If one wishes to define more clearly the ethical meaning of work, it is this truth that one must particularly keep in mind. (9)

> Work constitutes a foundation for the formation of family life, which is a natural right and something that man

is called to. . . . In a way, work is a condition for making it possible to found a family, since the family requires the means of subsistence which man normally gains through work. Work and industriousness also influence the whole process of education in the family, for the very reason that everyone "becomes a human being" through, among other things, work, and becoming a human being is precisely the main purpose of the whole process of education. (10)

. . . it [society] is also a great historical and social incarnation of the work of all generations. All of this brings it about that man combines his deepest human identity with membership of a nation, and intends his work also to increase the common good developed together with his compatriots, thus realizing that in this way work serves to add to the heritage of the whole human family, of all the people living in the world. (10)

The valuing process determines life. Values lead to an internal judgment which in turn dictates actions. The degree of worth we assign to individuals and things has far-reaching consequences. Within the complex valuing system, work plays a major role since it touches personal lives, family life, and even national and international communities. The value assigned to work in these three areas will affect, for good or ill, the course of history.

Family life remains a pivotal force in society. That life is threatened by an increasing number of divorces, the current mobility and the impact of the mass media. Unemployment is another threat which can lead to "social disaster." (18) Further, inadequate wages deprive the family of essential goods; lack of proper benefits increase anxiety; dissatisfaction with one's job has an impact on spouse and children.

Work has a wider circle than just family life—it influences all of society. When people are given proper job opportunities the common good is served and society is healthy. When work fosters a sense of cooperation among employees and employers, a new spirit of solidarity is felt in the wider society. When work is done so that future generations will be served and helped by conserving our resources and protecting our environment, society is being given responsible models. We have reached a point where this type of social consciousness can no longer remain merely a hope; if it does not become a fact, our society may well be doomed.

Few people can grow interiorly without a sense of achievement. When work is done well confidence and a sense of self-worth increase. Further, in fulfilling the commandment of God that we do work, we contribute to God's plan. The brick we add has eternal significance; no one else can do the work assigned to us. A prayer attributed to Cardinal Newman conveys the importance and the enigma of each person's work:

> God has created me to do Him some definite service;
> He has committed some work to me which He has not
> committed to another. I have my mission—I may
> never know it in this life, but I shall be told it
> in the next.

> I am like a link chain, a bond of connection between
> persons. He has not created me for naught. I shall
> do good, I shall do His work. I shall be an angel
> of peace, a preacher of truth in my own place while not
> intending it—if I do but keep His commandments.

> Therefore I will trust Him. Whatever, wherever I am,
> I can never be thrown away. If I am in sickness, my
> sickness may serve Him; in perplexity, my perplexity
> may serve Him; if I am in sorrow, my sorrow may serve Him.
> He does nothing in vain. He knows what He is about.
> He may take away my friends. He may throw me
> among strangers. He may hide my future from me—
> still He knows what He is about.

THEME 4: WORK AND THE MYSTERY OF CREATION

THESIS: *Work is inextricably bound up with the mystery of God's creative activity; each person shares in the wonder of creation through work.*

The knowledge that by means of work man shares in the work of creation constitutes the most profound motive for undertaking it in various sectors. (25)

In every phase of the development of his work man comes up against the leading role of the gift made by "nature," that is, in the final analysis, by the Creator. At the beginning of man's work is the mystery of creation. This affirmation, already indicated as my starting point, is the guiding thread of this document. (12)

The word of God's revelation is profoundly marked by the fundamental truth that man, created in the image of God, shares by his work in the activity of the Creator and that, within the limits of his own human capabilities, man in a sense continues to develop that activity, and perfects it as he advances further and further in the discovery of the resources and values contained in the whole of creation. (25)

Two qualities identify our humanness: dependence and creativity. All is gift and we have an absolute dependence on our Creator. Humble acceptance of these faith facts sets us free. Through the creative process order is extracted from chaos, unity is chiseled out of diversity, beauty is captured in stone, word or canvas. As Gerald Vann remarks:

The so-called industrial revolution ran its course; and ended by depriving the mass of men of a fundamental right, of that without which the personality is doomed to sterility and despair: the creativity which is the counterpart of creatureliness.[3]

Within these two qualities of our humanness is the duty and right of work.

Cooperation can be a most thrilling human experience. God longs for us to work with him in the fulfillment of the plan of salvation. Our very activity is an essential ingredient in the building of the earth and of the Kingdom! The dignity of such a mission is immeasurable. Yet that is precisely what our scriptural and theological understanding of work indicates: the people of God continue to share in the work of creation. The Vatican II document *Gaudium et Spes* drives home the reality that we are a Church *in* the modern world, an "in" that means involvement. Any mentality that either despises history or refuses to invest time and energy in improvement of the world goes contrary to the scriptures and the teaching of the Church.

Participation in the mystery of creation is threatened in our time. The buildup of armaments, sufficient now to many times over destroy our planet, leads many to an attitude of pessimism if not despair. Such a consciousness causes paralysis and the mission of work goes unaccomplished. The land is not tilled, books are not written, songs are not sung, families are not raised, conflicts are not resolved, resources are exploited. Why not? Annihilation is not only possible but likely! Suspicion is abroad: our times are less creative because of an annihilation attitude. Perhaps we can learn a lesson from Anne Frank. With bombs dropping near her hideout and with death a constant threat, she continued to study her history lesson. Life goes on! Christian faith calls us to our creative work regardless of the dark clouds that surround us. And, of course, one of the most urgent creative works is peace. Our work must bring about a world in which war becomes impossible.

THEME 5: A SPIRITUALITY OF WORK

THESIS: *Work is a means by which persons grow in union with God and participate in the paschal mystery.*

She [the Church] sees it as her particular duty to form a spirituality of work which will help all people to come closer, through work, to God, the Creator and Redeemer, to participate in his salvific plan for man and the world and to deepen their friendship with Christ in their lives by accepting, through faith, a living participation in his threefold mission as Priest, Prophet and King, as the Second Vatican Council so eloquently teaches. (24)

This Christian spirituality should be a heritage shared by all. Especially in the modern age, the spirituality of work should show the maturity called for by the tensions and restlessness of mind and heart. (25)

Since work in its subjective aspect is always a personal action, an *actus personae*, it follows that the whole person, body and spirit, participates in it, whether it is manual or intellectual work. It is also to the whole person that the word of the living God is directed, the evangelical message of salvation, in which we find many points which concern human work and which throw particular light on it. These points need to be properly assimilated: an inner effort on the part of the human spirit, guided by faith, hope and charity, is needed in order that through these points, the work of the individual human being may be given the meaning which it has in the eyes of God and by means of which work enters into the salvation process on a par with the other ordinary yet particularly important components of its texture. (24)

The farmer brings the seeds of the field to the Eucharist for a special blessing on rural life day, thereby exercising an act of faith in God as creator of the seed and provider for its growth. The newspaper editor cries out against the injustices toward the elderly thereby fulfilling his prophetic role of denouncing all that infringes upon human dignity and freedom. The president of a country, through policies that properly distribute funds, insures that the poor and needy have their due. The people of God are scattered throughout every profession and work situation and it is precisely in that context that they exercise their spirituality. Union with God is achieved not only through liturgical worship and the celebration of the sacraments. Holiness is gained as well by finding Christ in our brothers and sisters, in the working of the land, in our artistic and intellectual achievements. All of life, permeated by God's presence and love, becomes a graced opportunity and can further the process of salvation.

A spirituality of work demands three things: vision, grace and commitment. An abiding *vision* of the divine presence is a gift of faith. Work is not restricted to the narrow sensate culture (limiting work to the confines of time/space) nor to a humanistic betterment of the world, important as that is. Rather, faith vision situates our work as an integral part of God's salvific will. *Grace*, the free gift of God's self-giving which transforms our minds and hearts, is the heartbeat of a spirituality for work. Empowered by the Spirit, our work has a certain quality and tonality that makes everything different. There is a freshness, newness and sense of possibility in what is done. Eventually the work will incarnate that grace as another sign of God's favor. Further, *commitment* to the person of Christ by sharing in his life, death and resurrection undergirds all Christian spirituality. The paschal mystery draws us into the dying/rising process of Christian existence. Work constantly involves dying and rising; done in union with Christ it allows us to become the person God calls us to be.

In *Zorba the Greek*, Nikos Kazantzakis has one of the characters describe his experience, "I at last realized that eating was a spiritual function and that meat, bread and wine were the raw materials from which the mind is made."[4] No longer is there a harsh dichotomy between the secular and the sacred, the flesh and the spirit, heaven and earth. A false dualism is rejected and the unity of existence maintained. Work and worship are not mutually exclusive; they are meant to complement and enrich one another. For some workers their highest moments of prayerful praise and thanksgiving are in the midst of their work experience. A mother caring for her child, the artist sharing his masterpiece, the nurse weeping with the terminally ill, the scientist discovering a new atomic particle, the scholar articulating an insight: nurturing, creating, caring, wondering, discovering, sharing—moments of work, grounded in sacrifice, discipline and great effort, AND moments of grace. All of this contributes to a spirituality of work because to live in God's presence with sensitivity, awareness and love is to live a spiritual life.

THEME 6: WORK AND QUESTIONS OF JUSTICE
THESIS: *Work plays a significant function in the justice question; there can be no justice unless work is available to people in such a way that basic rights and duties are protected and promoted.*

> In order to achieve social justice in the various parts of the world, in the various countries, and in the relationships between them, there is need for ever new movements of solidarity of the workers and with the workers. This solidarity must be present whenever it is called for by the social degrading of the subject of work, by exploitation of the workers, and by the growing areas of poverty and hunger. (8)

> It must be stressed that the constitutive element in this progress and also the most adequate way to verify it in a spirit of justice and peace, which the Church proclaims and for which she does not cease to pray to the Father of all individuals and of all peoples, is the continual reappraisal of man's work, both in the aspect of its objective finality and in the aspect of the dignity of the subject of all work, that is to say, man. The progress in

question must be made through man and for man and it must produce its fruit in man. A test of this progress will be the increasingly mature recognition of the purpose of work and increasingly universal respect for the rights inherent in work in conformity with the dignity of man, the subject of work. (18)

While work, in all its many senses, is an obligation, that is to say a duty, it is also a source of rights on the part of the worker. These rights must be examined in the broad context of human rights as a whole, which are connatural with man, and many of which are proclaimed by various international organizations and increasingly guaranteed by the individual States for their citizens. Respect for this broad range of human rights constitutes the fundamental condition for peace in the modern world. (16)

Whenever relationships are established, certain issues of justice automatically arise. By its very definition the work relationship between employer and employee presents a mutuality of duties and rights. The encyclical addresses itself primarily to threatened rights of the employee, giving little attention to the duties of the employee toward the employer. Employees' rights are numerous: the right to a just wage, the right to social benefits to ensure life and health, the right to rest, the right to pension and insurance, the right to suitable working environments, the right to strike under certain circumstances, the right to form voluntary associations, the right of the disabled to productive activity suited to them, the right to emigrate in search of work. The correlative list would include the duties that come to the employer or society because of these rights. This area of justice is specific and measurable; much honesty, dialogue and planning is necessary if the ideal is to be achieved.

The linkage between justice and peace is clearly articulated:

Commitment to justice must be closely linked with
commitment to peace in the modern world. (2)

Respect for this broad range of human rights constitutes the
fundamental condition for peace in the modern world. (16)

Whenever rights are denied or duties neglected, a profound disturbance shakes the life of individuals and society
at large. Theologically we call this "sin," ethically we call it
"injustice," sociologically we call it "alienation." Regardless
of the language system, the experience and its consequences
are clear: the order of God's plan is broken and until reconciliation comes about, until justice is done, the fragmentation continues and peace is not found in the land. Mere
absence of war or conflict is not peace; rather, it is an
ontological state of being, experienced when relationships
are properly ordered.

If charity begins at home, all the more so justice. Thus
the Church as an institution must constantly strive for
justice and peace within her own immediate membership.
The fact that the above rights reside in her own personnel
imposes an obligation on the Church as employer. This
"beginning at home" is significant since authenticity of
teaching and preaching constantly seeks verification in
practice. When the Church both teaches justice and lives it,
the world has a model which affirms that the realities of
justice and peace are truly possible.

THEME 7: WORK AND VARIOUS IDEOLOGIES

THESIS: *Work demands a meaning and various interpretations
are offered by Liberalism, Marxism and Christian
theology.*

The Marxist programme, based on the philosophy of
Marx and Engels, sees in class struggle the only way to
eliminate class injustices in society and to eliminate the

classes themselves. Putting this programme into practice presupposes the collectivization of the means of production so that, through the transfer of these means from private hands to the collectivity, human labor will be preserved from exploitation. (11)

This consistent image, in which the principle of the primacy of person over things is strictly preserved, was broken up in human thought, sometimes after a long period of incubation in practical living. The break occurred in such a way that labor was separated from capital and set in opposition to it, and capital was set in opposition to labor, as though they were two impersonal forces, two production factors juxtaposed in the same "economistic" perspective. This way of stating the issue contained a fundamental error, what we call the error of economism, that of considering human labor solely according to its economic purpose. This fundamental error of thought can and must be called an error of materialism, in that economism directly or indirectly includes a conviction of the primacy and superiority of the material, and directly or indirectly places the spiritual and the personal [man's activity, moral values and such matters] in a position of subordination to material reality. (13)

The only chance there seems to be for radically overcoming this error [primitive capitalism and liberalism] is through adequate changes both in theory and in practice, changes in line with the definite conviction of the primacy of the person over things, and of human labor over capital as a whole collection of means of production. (13)

Absolutizing is that radical instinct in thought and behavior that makes one idea or value the *only* idea or value. The label we attach to such a tendency is "isms": e.g. *secularism* holds that all reality is limited to this world—there is no transcendence; *humanism* measures all of life in the light of the human person—God finds no home here; *rationalism* restricts valid knowledge to that gained by reason—faith vision is excluded; *workism* so prizes achievement and productivity that leisure (receptivity-contemplation) is meaningless if not downright evil. The encyclical deals with this proclivity to absolutize and firmly rejects certain specific "isms" that surround work. *Anathema sit*: *Marxism* that seeks a *collectivism* of means of production so as to infringe upon the right to private property; *liberalism* that fails to take into account the common good in its worship of primitive *capitalism*; *economism* that views human labor solely in terms of its economic purposes; *materialism* that subordinates the spiritual/personal aspects of life to material reality.

Christian theology consistently seeks a balanced position that protects moral and personal and spiritual values. Thus private property is a basic right, though the common good will severely limit this right or even exclude it under very restricted circumstances. Economic profit is necessary and justifiable but never at the expense of human dignity. Matter is part of God's creation but is subordinated to the value of the human person. The insights of scripture and tradition are brought to bear upon the complex reality of the work world. Basic principles are articulated through careful theological reflection which provides a theory that will hopefully inform our action. The Church is not reluctant to speak out with a strong prophetic voice whenever there is encroachment upon the rights of people, be that encroachment by employer or employee.

Jacob Bronowski states that "without astronomy it is really not possible to find your way over great distances, or even to have a theory about the shape of the earth and the land and sea on it."[5] Part of the Church's mission is to provide a theological astronomy by which the complex components of life can be assessed and prudently judged. The present papal document serves a timely purpose: it articulates a theology and a spirituality from which to observe and practice the command of God that we work, thereby building up a more human community and furthering the growth of the Kingdom. Such an astronomy is no luxury, it is an absolute necessity.

THEME 8: WORK AND ITS ABUSE
THESIS: *Work, which is meant to humanize and develop persons, can become destructive when means become ends.*

> . . . it [the antinomy between labor and capital] originated in the whole of the economic and social practice of that time, the time of the birth and rapid development of industrialization, in which what was mainly seen was the possibility of vastly increasing material wealth, means, while the end, that is to say, man, who should be served by the means, was ignored. (13)

> The primary basis of the value of work is man himself, who is its subject. This leads immediately to a very important conclusion of an ethical nature: however true it may be that man is destined for work and called to it, in the first place work is "for man" and not man "for work." (6)

> The very process of "subduing the earth," that is to say work, is marked in the course of history and especially in recent centuries, by an immense development of technological means. This is an advantageous and positive phenomenon, on condition that the objective dimension of work does not gain the upper hand over the subjective dimension, depriving man of his dignity and inalienable rights or reducing them. (10)

A Gospel question focuses our attention: is man made for the Sabbath or the Sabbath for man? Jesus had to deal with the means/end question and there is nothing unclear about his answer: the Sabbath is made for man. Ambiguity characterizes some contemporary questions arising from the world of work: What is the relationship between technology and the human person? What status does the individual have in large multinational corporations? When transfers are made, what considerations are given to the worker's family? If profits will be less but the work situation is more humanizing, what kinds of decisions are made? Is man made for work or work for man? Historically the document states that certain means have usurped the prerogatives of the end; technology (means) has become the master and the human person (end), the slave. At this juncture, justice and peace are no more. The whole order is overturned, human freedom is lost.

Simone Weil, a strong prophetic voice for the value of work in the first half of this century, worked in factories so as to experientially learn the worker's situation. Her experience was not a happy one: workers were dehumanized because they were treated simply as cogs in a large, productive machine. Upon reading Homer's *Iliad*, she extracts a universal truth about evil that applies to our present discussion:

> Thus in this ancient and wonderful poem there already appeared the essential evil besetting humanity, the substitution of means for ends.[6]

What is so horrendous is that often this process of evil is unconscious and unintended. The means we use for productivity are happily introduced. Suddenly we wake up one morning and come to realize that we are controlled by the very process we devised.

The underlying question is one of freedom, a freedom that protects our humanity and a freedom to use tools of production wisely. Such a freedom comes only from hard-won knowledge: we cannot make prudent choices when ignorant of facts and circumstances. Education is of greatest importance here. All people involved in the working community must maintain a high level of attentiveness to attitudes, means of production, societal tendencies, subtle shifts in values. The means/end dilemma must not be blurred. Melville, in his classic *Moby Dick*, comments that "ignorance is the parent of fear."[7] Societal fears often arise because we are ignorant of the proper relationship between means and end. With increased knowledge we are hopeful that fear will be dissipated and our freedom regained.

THEME 9: WORK AND THE COMMON GOOD
THESIS: *Work, through the use of natural and personal resources, is an essential force to achieve the common good.*

> . . . society—even when it has not yet taken on the mature form of a nation—is not only the great "educator" of every man, even though an indirect one (because each individual absorbs within the family the contents and values that go to make up the culture of a given nation); it is also a great historical and social incarnation of the work of all generations. All of this brings it about that man combines his deepest human identity with membership of a nation, and intends his work also to increase the common good developed together with his compatriots, thus realizing that in this way work serves to add to the heritage of the whole human family, of all the people living in the world. (16)

> Rational planning and the proper organization of human labor in keeping with individual societies and States should also facilitate the discovery of the right proportions between the different kinds of employment: work on the land, in industry, in the various services, white-collar work and scientific or artistic work, in accordance with the capacities of individuals; and for the common good of each society and of the whole of mankind. (18)

> Here we must return once more to the first principle of the whole ethical and social order, namely, the principle

of the common use of goods. In every system, regardless of the fundamental relationships within it between capital and labor, wages, that is to say remuneration for work, are still a practical means whereby the vast majority of people have access to those goods which are intended for common use: both the goods of nature and manufactured goods. (19)

In the document *Gaudium et Spes*, the fathers of the Second Vatican Council described the common good in these terms:

Now, the common good embraces the sum of those conditions of social life by which individuals, families and groups can achieve their own fulfillment in a relatively thorough and ready way. (74)

Although somewhat nebulous in the abstract, the common good is extremely concrete and pragmatic in experience. Yet certain cultural attitudes towards private goods and vested self-interest make it difficult for the relationship between work and the common good to be properly understood. One such attitude regards common good items (parks, public buildings, etc.) as areas of exploitation, with no sense of personal responsibility for their upkeep or cleanliness. A mentality of privatized ownership threatens the realization of the common good. Through work I will take as much as I can without any thought of making my contribution to the commonweal. Various writers[8] are beginning to articulate a public theology and notions of a public Church which help to provide a vision for the protection of the common good through responsible work and concern.

Several years ago there was a global experience that had the potentiality to develop social consciousness for the common good. For the first time in history, through the technology of cameras, we saw ourselves, the planet earth, from the moon. Hurling through space like people on a small raft, this brought us a realization that we are all in this together. The activity of one affects the activity of all. Responsible work and sharing enriches the human family; failure to do so diminishes and deprives people of quality life. Perhaps the moon photograph has been blurred already and the strong sense of interdependence to which we are called has been obscured by innate avariciousness. Is work done primarily for profit and personal gain? Have we forgotten the common good or disregarded it as some utopian dream?

Two types of people have been known throughout history as truly human and noble: people of compassion and people of hospitality. The former have a heart that is moved deeply by the joy and sufferings of others. A basic affinity with human experience resides deep within the being of compassionate people. Hospitality, that gracious welcoming of the stranger into personal space and time, creates an environment in which the common good is realized. Regardless of one's employment, the works of compassion and hospitality are universal vocations and only when they are exercised, thus producing the common good, do individual goods have any value whatever. The paradox of the gospel grain of wheat is lived again.

THEME 10: WORK AND COMMUNITY

THESIS: *Work builds community by uniting people into a powerful solidarity.*

> In fact, the family is simultaneously a community made possible by work and the first school of work, within the home, for every person. (10)

> The call to solidarity and common action addressed to the worker—especially to those engaged in narrowly specialized, monotonous and depersonalized work in industrial plants, when the machine tends to dominate

man—was important and eloquent from the point of view of social ethics. It was the reaction against the degradation of man as the subject of work, and against the unheard-of accompanying exploitation in the fields of wages, working conditions and social security for the worker. This reaction united the working world in a community marked by great solidarity. (8)

It is characteristic of work that it first and foremost unites people. In this consists its social power: the power to build a community. In the final analysis, both those who work and those who manage the means of production or who own them must in some way be united in this community. (20)

Communities are formed when there is a common sense of identity, when there is a commitment to a specific value system, when lives are shared by mutual experience. Many work situations have these three qualities. A good school faculty know who they are, are committed to truth and its various expressions, and share lives professionally and, to some degree, socially. A professional sports team working together for several years establishes a strong communal bond. Work has the potential to unite people and form community, i.e., a style of work that is balanced and person centered. What is intriguing is that often the bond of community happens without conscious planning; it is a side effect of deep cooperation.

Human life is complex. Like a spider's web, there are many intersecting lines in our relationships and in our multiple communities, e.g.,

The community to which I belong is, of course, not a static one. Sometimes it is the community of my wife and myself and my family; at other times that of my relations, of my friends, of my work colleagues, of my city or nation or international grouping. My task in each different community varies according to the particular community I am being consciously part of at any time. In some communities, I am a key figure; in others, of lesser or minimal importance. But in all of them I have a function, a duty and a responsibility and I believe I will be judged on my performance of these at the end of my time. Often I do not know exactly what that function is—but I know that basically it is to be a harmonizing influence, a peacemaker, a go-between, a catalyst, a bringer-out of good qualities in others for the sake of a group.[9]

This vision of community and work depicts the range of groupings in one's life and the specific functions that we are to play. The notion of facilitator may accurately describe "the work" (the process of life itself) that will build any community. We facilitate relationships by bringing love and concern which, in turn, bring about peace and oneness.

The Gospel of John states that God is always working. Jesus presents himself as *the waiter*, serving at table those who come for life-giving food. The thrust behind this work is community, to build and complete the Father's Kingdom. Thus the dignity of the vocation of work becomes clear: as co-worker with the Lord we participate in the process of reconciliation, bringing all creation back to the Father. Whatever our task in life, however sublime or humble, we lovingly accept the charge given us and contribute to the realization of the Father's plan. *Adveniat regnum!*

Footnotes

1. "The American Scholar," in *The Selected Writings of Ralph Waldo Emerson*, ed. Brooks Atkinson (New York: The Modern Library, 1940), 55.
2. *Meister Eckhart*, trans. Raymond B. Blakney (New York: Harper Torchbooks, 1941), 87.
3. Gerald Vann, *St. Thomas Aquinas* (New York: Benziger Bros., 1947), 27.
4. Nikos Kazantzakis, *Zorba the Greek* (New York: Simon and Schuster, 1952), 79.
5. Jacob Bronowski, *The Ascent of Man* (Boston: Little, Brown and Company, 1973), 190.

6. *The Simone Weil Reader*, ed. George A. Panichas (New York: David McKay Company, Inc., 1977), 138.
7. Herman Melville, *Moby Dick* (New York: The Literary Guild of America, Inc., 1949), 17.
8. See Martin E. Marty's *The Public Church* (New York: Crossroad, 1981) and Parker J. Palmer's *The Company of Strangers* (New York: Crossroad, 1981).
9. *On the Run: Spirituality for the Seventies*, ed. by Michael F. McCauley (Chicago: The Thomas More Association, 1974), 138.

FAMILIARIS CONSORTIO:
Themes and Theses

On November 22, 1981, Pope John Paul II issued an apostolic exhortation *Familiaris Consortio*. This document on the family followed the Synod of Bishops meeting that dealt at length with issues of family life. A vast range of topics was discussed: (1) the role of the family—its identity and mission. The centrality of love was stressed with great clarity. (2) The meaning of human sexuality, meaning which can be found only when sexuality is perceived in relationship to the whole person and to the plan of God. (3) The call to the family to participate in the development of society. This challenge prevents a narrow parochialism and urges a social consciousness that is inclusive. (4) The character of rights for the family. Without justice there will be no peace in the home or among nations. (5) Concern for the hurting. Compassion demands that we reach out to the families that are broken and experiencing loss of any kind.

Documents such as this exhortation serve a most important purpose in life, i.e., the sharing of a vision. Parker J. Palmer writes of the need for vision:

> Finally, we need to seek and find the grounds of Christian hope in the midst of our public crisis. Those grounds are to be found in God's promise of reconciliation and God's faithfulness to that promise. We will touch that ground and root ourselves in it through prayer and contemplation—not as an

isolated individual act, but as directed and disciplined within the community of faith. Just as private and public life are halves of a larger whole, so private prayer and public worship are meant to be as one.

In all these ways the church can help renew that vision without which the people perish![1]

In a society that is pluralistic, in a world ajar with great changes, in a Church undergoing rapid development, the vision of the family is bound to be obscured. Whatever can help clarify the basic elements of family life and its interdependence with the Church and society is invaluable in daily decision making. *Familiaris Consortio* provides a vision from which to evaluate and plan.

Unfortunately, because of its length, this document may well find its way to the shelf unmarked and unread, suffering the same fate as *Pacem in Terris*, *Laborem Exercens*, and *Redemptor Hominis*. If this happens, the vision remains at a certain level of leadership but never gets into the minds and the hearts of the people. The problem is one of communication. This chapter attempts to give a general overview of the central themes of the document; its aim is to attract the reader to the primary source itself.

THEME 1: FAMILY

THESIS: *The Christian Family is a community of persons committed to self-giving and fidelity.*

The family, which is founded and given life by love, is a community of persons: of husband and wife, of parents and children, of relatives. Its first task is to live with fidelity the reality of communion in a constant effort to develop an authentic community of persons. (18)

The family is the first and fundamental school of social living: as a community of love, it finds in self-giving the law that guides it and makes it grow. The self-giving that inspires the love of husband and wife for each other is the model and norm for the self-giving that must be practiced in the relationships between brothers and sisters and the different generations living together in the family. And the communion and sharing that are part of everyday life in the home at times of joy and at times of difficulty are the most concrete and effective pedagogy for the active, responsible and fruitful inclusion of the children in the wider horizon of society. (37)

Loving the family means being able to appreciate its values and capabilities, fostering them always. Loving the family means identifying the dangers and the evils that menace it, in order to overcome them. Loving the family means endeavoring to create for it an environment favorable for its development. (86)

In his strong and sensitive novel *A Death in the Family*, James Agee writes of the delicate bonds of family life. Those bonds were ruptured when the father of the family was killed in a car accident. His son Rufus cries out to his mother: "Hideandseek's just a game, just a game. God doesn't fool around playing games, does He, Mama! Does He!" The story paints the intersecting lines of relatives and friends offering sympathy and advice, raising questions and sharing consolation. A community of persons dealing with life and death, faith and doubt, joy and sorrow. A family at once imbued with love and yet wrenched with selfishness. Agee masterfully tells of people striving to sustain relationships in adverse circumstances, striving to comprehend life in the face of death. This finely tuned story provides an example of family life; the apostolic exhortation addresses itself to such a community and offers a faith perspective for dealing with life's questions.

The backbone of family life is community. When a group of people live out a common value system in which each individual is deeply loved and challenged, a oneness is formed which we call community. It is more a process than a state of being. Its organic nature means that things never remain the same. This constant flux is not to be understood negatively. Rather, this positive change is called growth, the development which underlies every healthy family. The values are constant, their implementation and application continue to vary. Community happens when people truly care and share. The central act of the family and community is self-giving: the ability to be with and for others in a loving and compassionate way. This act is not without its risks. While it can and often does lead to acceptance, such sharing can also lead to rejection. Relationships demand trust, that invisible elixir, which creates an atmosphere in which dialogue and revelation can happen. Where do we find authentic family life? Where self-giving, trust, sharing and love abide!

The prophets confronted the people with the sin that destroyed the family of Israel: infidelity! Hosea would say: "My people are diseased through their disloyalty" (Ho 11:7). The haunting motto *semper fidelis* must not be ignored. Family life and community depend upon depth commitment that is able to withstand the fierce testing of crises and weaknesses. Much grace is needed, especially in a culture that accepts infidelity as being "only human." Humorously if sadly, we speak about a dog as being man's best friend—yet the fidelity of a dog does at times outrun human commitment. Often the apostolic document draws our attention to the power, necessity and beauty of fidelity.

THEME 2: SACRAMENT OF MARRIAGE

THESIS: *The sacrament of marriage is God's special grace enlightening a couple to see their true vocation and empowering them to live it.*

The gift of the sacrament is at the same time a vocation and commandment for the Christian spouses, that they may remain faithful to each other forever, beyond every trial and difficulty, in generous obedience to the holy will of the Lord: "What therefore God has joined together, let not man put asunder." (20)

A vivid and attentive awareness of the mission that they have received with the sacrament of marriage will help Christian parents to place themselves at the service of their children's education with great serenity and trustfulness, and also with a sense of responsibility before God, who calls them and gives them the mission of building up the Church in their children. Thus in the case of baptized people, the family, called together by word and sacrament as the Church of the home, is both teacher and mother, the same as the world-wide Church. (38)

The social role that belongs to every family pertains by a new and original right to the Christian family, which is based on the sacrament of marriage. By taking up the human reality of the love between husband and wife in all its implications, the sacrament gives to Christian couples and parents a power and commitment to live their vocation as lay people and therefore to "seek the kingdom of God by engaging in temporal affairs and by ordering them according to the plan of God." (47)

The sacrament of marriage is the specific source and original means of sanctification for Christian married couples and families. It takes up again and makes specific the sanctifying grace of Baptism. (56)

God is love! In divine self-giving we receive that love which we call grace. Faith allows us to experience the mystery that God has made his home in our hearts, that we are indeed temples of the Spirit. As blood flows through our systems providing life and energy, so grace flows through life affording participation in the Divine Reality. Freely given, it must be freely accepted and exercised. Such gifted-ness does impose serious demands on the individual and the community. Because of this there is a tendency to resist the reception of God's love and to opt for that "cheap grace" which seemingly makes no demands. Such a choice is fatal because it is a lie. Grace will always remain true to its essence: love calling out to love. Once received it must be shared lest one's very integrity be shattered.

Grace comes to married life and love through the sacrament of marriage in a very special way. This visible sign of God's incomprehensible love brings about what it signifies: union and holiness. Such is the vocation for all people. God provides specific help to couples who have special demands in the nurturing and sustaining of unique relationships. The sacrament has two sides: invitation and imperative. By means of the invitation each couple builds up the Church and by fulfilling the imperative they participate in the work of salvation. In order that this be known and deeply sensed, the apostolic exhortation stresses the significance of adequate preparation. An understanding of the meaning of grace, as well as the invitation and imperative that underlies it, is crucial to successful married life. Proper disposition makes possible a full response. Here, as in most situations, ignorance is not bliss.

Anwar el-Sadat, in his autobiography *In Search of Identity*, reflects on a central question of life, one's vocation:

> Without a vocation, man's existence would be meaningless. We have been created to bear the responsibility God has entrusted us with. Though different, each man should fulfill his specific vocation and shoulder his individual responsibility.[2]

Marriage is a vocation, one sanctified by a sacrament. God's calling is accompanied by the necessary help enabling an adequate response in the light of one's gifts and talents. A sense of identity enriches family life and interpersonal relationships. Without this self-awareness, the inner poverty of relationships results in destructive deprivation. Only a sense of one's vocation allows for the proper ordering of life's many demands. Marriage as a basic vocation claims centrality: work, play and social engagements all take a secondary role. A constant challenge in life is to get in touch with one's vocation and to maintain an abiding awareness of this mystery.

THEME 3: MISSION/TASK OF THE FAMILY
THESIS: *Christian families are called to receive and share the divine graces of life and love.*

> Looking at it in such a way as to reach its very roots we must say that the essence and role of the family are in the final analysis specified by love. Hence the family has *the mission to guard, reveal and communicate love*, and this is a living reflection of and a real sharing in God's love for humanity and the love of Christ the Lord for the Church his bride. (17)

> Thus, with love as its point of departure and making constant reference to it, the recent Synod emphasized four general tasks for the family:
> (1) forming a community of persons;
> (2) serving life;
> (3) participating in the development of society;
> (4) sharing in the life and mission of the Church. (17)

> Therefore love and life constitute the nucleus of the saving mission of the Christian family in the Church and for the Church. (50)

A movie, a novel, or a walk through Disneyland often offers a moment of escape from the harsher realities of life. In the film *Raiders of the Lost Ark* impossible missions are pulled off one after another. Sheer enjoyment, totally unreal. After such moments we re-enter the real world: the world of work, the world of international conflict, the world of the family. Missions here seem impossible as well: to bring about justice, to foster peace, to live love. Indeed, without grace and great personal effort the task is overwhelming, if not impossible; with discipline and divine assistance the ideals of justice, peace and love become historical realities.

Authors from various disciplines have constantly commented on the task and mission of the family: love and life.

> A father did not visit his son, nor the son his father. Charity was dead.[3]

> I've always been intense about relationships. At times, my love overwhelms people. And it puzzles me. My business is to love.[4]

> . . . and Alyosha's heart could not endure uncertainty because his love was always of an active character. He was incapable of passive love. If he loved anyone, he set to work at once to love him.[5]

Thus writes Barbara Tuchman in her excellent study *A Distant Mirror*; in *The Belle of Amherst* playwright William Luce puts words into the mouth of Emily Dickinson; Dostoevsky too ponders the movements and the mystery of love in his character Alyosha. There is a certain messiness in the mission. Oftentimes motives are mixed in trying to love. Grace faces blockages and detours at every turn. Infrequent success and daily failures can be discouraging. Yet the moments of concern, care, respect and love—the central vocation of the human heart—are breakthroughs of healing, redemptive life. The exhortation strikes dead center in urging families to guard love from every danger, to reveal love in trust and openness, to communicate love through honest dialogue. The mission is realized by means of such activity.

Four specific tasks are delineated for the family: (1) The mission of forming interpersonal relationships, of building community. Such formation demands time and self-giving; it is endangered by loss of identity and ambiguity about central values. (2) The mission of serving life by protecting the procreative and unitive functions of married love. Education and ongoing training are also tasks of parents. (3) The mission of participating in societal and political changes of society. Reaching out to the larger community prevents a destructive individualism. (4) The mission of becoming Church. Through love Christ is made present in our homes and in our world.

THEME 4: LOVE
THESIS: *The heartbeat and central principle of family life is love.*

> God is love and in himself he lives a mystery of personal loving communion. Creating the human race in his own image and continually keeping it in being, God inscribed in the humanity of man and woman the vocation, and thus the capacity and responsibility, of love and communion. Love is therefore the fundamental and innate vocation of every human being. (11)

> The inner principle of that task [to develop an authentic community of persons], its permanent power and its final goal is love: without love the family is not a community of persons and, in the same way, *without love the family cannot live, grow and perfect itself as a community of persons.* (18)

> It cannot be forgotten that the most basic element, so basic that it qualifies the educational role of parents, is *parental love*, which finds fulfillment in the task of education as it completes and perfects its service of life: as well as being a *source*, the parent's love is also the *animating principle* and therefore the *norm* inspiring and guiding all concrete educational activity, enriching it with the values of kindness, constancy, goodness, service, disinterestedness, and self-sacrifice that are the most precious fruit of love. (36)

Vocation is a mystery. Who can explain exactly how a call comes into our lives and what makes it possible to respond? Faith offers some reflections on this matter and the Second Vatican Council clearly states that all people are called to holiness. The present document says the same thing but in a different way: the intrinsic calling of every person is love. How this universal vocation is lived out is determined by the specific path an individual chooses: single life, married life, religious life. In a sense there is both freedom and determination here. We are free to choose our unique path, we are not free not to be loving and still retain our humanity. Romano Guardini understood well the process involved in discerning one's vocation:

> A vocation is no label marked "chosen" which can be fixed to a human existence once and forever. It is a living intention of God, efficacy of his love in the chosen one. Only through the action taken by that person can it become reality.[6]

The family is inextricably involved in the vocation question. The pragmatic "how" question arises in the search for love and community within the family circle. Many forces that tend to block love and concern must be dealt with. How can we live simple and fruitful lives in a culture characterized by chaos and violence? The good news of the Gospel draws our attention to the person of Jesus in whom we find love incarnate. The basic command is not merely a verbal communication—it is a lived reality. Before preaching Jesus so often heals, frees, forgives—only then does he explain in word what has taken place. Such self-giving is the model for the family, the domestic Church. Jesus shares with that Church his Spirit that enables her members to fulfill the perfect command to be loving, forgiving people. And within all this is a paradox: "Jesus' authentic power is revealed in his frailty and impotence."[7] The power of powerlessness lies at the heart of love, at the heart of the family.

Roots determine fruits. Where authentic parental love exists as the source of family life, then the possibility of various virtues finding expression in the lives of its members is probable. The apostolic exhortation lists six: (1) *Kindness*: that attitude and action that affirms and strengthens another; (2) *Constancy*: that rich fidelity fostering trust; (3) *Goodness*: love incarnate in a small word, a gracious deed; (4) *Service*: awareness of and response to the needs of others; (5) *Disinterestedness*: that unique self-forgetfulness in being for and with others; (6) *Self-sacrifice*: that realism that all love involves a cross. The vocation to love and to be loved is fulfilled only in grace.

THEME 5: SEXUALITY

THESIS: *Sexuality finds its full meaning only when seen in the context of the human person, God's plan and love.*

Consequently, sexuality, by means of which man and woman give themselves to one another through the acts which are proper and exclusive to spouses, is by no means something purely biological, but concerns the innermost being of the human person as such. It is realized in a truly human way only if it is an integral part of the love by which a man and a woman commit themselves totally to one another until death. The total physical self-giving would be a lie if it were not the sign and fruit of a total personal self-giving, in which the whole person, including the temporal dimension, is present: if the person were to withhold something or reserve the possibility of deciding otherwise in the future, by this very fact he or she would not be giving totally. (11)

In the context of a culture which seriously distorts or entirely misinterprets the true meaning of human sexuality, because it separates it from its essential reference to the person, the Church more urgently feels how irreplaceable is her mission of presenting sexuality as a

value and task of the whole person, created male and
female in the image of God. (32)

Education in love as self-giving is also the indispensable
premise for parents called to give their children a clear
and delicate *sex education*. Faced with a culture that
largely reduces human sexuality to the level of something commonplace, since it interprets and lives it in a
reductive and impoverished way by linking it solely with
the body and with selfish pleasure, the educational
service of parents must aim firmly at a training in the
area of sex that is truly and fully personal: for sexuality is
an enrichment of the whole person—body, emotions
and soul—and it manifests its inmost meaning in leading the person to the gift of self in love. (37)

When things are disconnected they become distorted.
The absolutizing tendency to identify a part for the whole is
not uncommon. A recent movie/play, *The Elephant Man*,
demonstrates what happens when a single element of life
excludes other facts. Most people were unable to move
beyond the elephant man's deformity and penetrate to the
rich, inner beauty of his person. Sexuality has suffered over
the years from the absolutizing impulse that has fragmented
this great and powerful gift. When sexuality is reduced to
physicality, emotionality or pleasure, meaning is lost.
Familiaris Consortio presents a different vision. Here sexuality is understood as an integral part of the personality. It has
meaning only in reference to the person and authentic love.
This integral vision provides meaning and allows for pru-
dential decision on how the gift will be used. Vision and
virtue help to order this radical power in our lives. Though
complex, sexuality is not incomprehensible; though in-
nately powerful, sexuality is not uncontrollable.

Certain things in history are a matter of life and death.
One of these is human sexuality. Abundant life flows when
this gift of sexuality is used with proper regard for the

individual and is an expression of authentic love. Physical, emotional and spiritual life are all enriched. However, when sexuality is misused and becomes a form of manipulation or exploitation, few things are as destructive. Death is the consistent effect of the unprincipled use of human sexuality. Here truth is abandoned, a lie is lived. The fruits are well known: deception, secretiveness, joylessness, angst, boredom—exit Mrs. Robinson. Thus the paradox: that which can be most life-giving is capable of causing infinite harm.

Sex education is an urgent need today. This obligation is frustrated because of confusion in regard to sexual matters, breakdown in communication, sheer neglect. Much information regarding sexual matters is transmitted through the mass media and peer groups, often highly distorted and erroneous. Justice is at stake. The child has the right to know; the duty rests primarily on parents. Assistance is often needed and other bodies (church and schools) get involved. One point must be stressed:

> . . . the Church is firmly opposed to an often widespread form of imparting sex information dissociated from moral principle. (37)

The key issue is clear: human sexuality must always be dealt with in context: the context of love, the human person and God's plan.

THEME 6: EDUCATION

THESIS: *Education is a primary duty and right of parents; the full growth and development of children depend upon the exercise of this obligation.*

> The task of giving education is rooted in the primary vocation of married couples to participate in God's creative activity: by begetting in love and for love a new

person who has within himself or herself the vocation to growth and development, parents by that very fact take on the task of helping that person effectively to live a fully human life. (36)

According to the plan of God, marriage is the foundation of the wider community of the family, since the very institution of marriage and conjugal love are ordained to the procreation and education of children, in whom they find their crowning. (14)

The mission to educate demands that Christian parents should present to their children all the topics that are necessary for the gradual maturing of their personality from a Christian and ecclesial point of view. They will therefore follow the educational lines mentioned above, taking care to show their children the depths of significance to which the faith and love of Jesus Christ can lead. (39)

Full growth and development demand education. This process of learning is of special significance in the first decade of a person's life. Here the twig is bent, the fate of the tree deeply influenced. In the confines of the home a type of informal education is always at work. By osmosis children are assimilating the values, thoughts and life style of their parents. There will be times of more formal education: planned discussion, structured dialogue, explicit exchange of facts and perspectives. Whether formal or informal, the learning process nourishes the mind and heart as food does the body. Intellectual needs are as deep as bodily ones. If deprived of proper feeding, strange compensatory behavior sets in, causing serious disorder of relationships. If nourishment is well balanced, the result is a healthy home and society.

Given the limitations of time, talent and skills, parents will necessarily reach out to others for help in the fulfillment of this primary obligation to educate their children. This appeal for help should not lead to abdication. Certain things can only be learned in the home: the art of sustaining relationships in close quarters, the ability to deal with moods over long periods of time, the gift of hospitality to strangers. In these and other areas, parents are always teaching, if not in word, certainly by their actions. To succeed in this duty parents must continue their own education. The formation of parents through information and transformation is necessary for the full development of the family.

In an age of rapid change and high activism, there is a special lesson that parents can teach their children, the lesson of silence:

> We have yet to accept and act upon the axiom that the cultivation of a habit of silence is an integral part of all true education; and that children, so far from looking upon a demand for silence as an unnatural and intolerable imposition, have an inborn aptitude for quietness.[8]

Such silence gives access to the voice of God and the deeper recesses of oneself. Contemplation then becomes a possibility and this activity is essential to a full, human life. Constant activity and incessant noise destroy the conditions for true humanness: loving attention and presence to others. A quiet period in the day could well be one of the greatest blessings a child might learn from parents and the home.

THEME 7: SOCIETY

THESIS: *The mutual relationship between family and society must be carefully nurtured and lovingly critiqued.*

The family has vital and organic links with society, since it is its foundation and nourishes it continually through its role of service to life: it is from the family that citizens come to birth and it is within the family that they find the first school of the social virtues that are the animating principle of the existence and development of society itself. (42)

The social role of families is called upon to find expression also in the form of *political intervention*: families should be the first to take steps to see that the laws and institutions of the State not only do not offend but support and positively defend the rights and duties of the family. Along these lines, families should grow in awareness of being "protagonists" of what is known as "family politics" and assume responsibility for transforming society; otherwise families will be the first victims of the evils that they have done no more than note with indifference. The Second Vatican Council's appeal to go beyond an individualistic ethic therefore also holds good for the family as such. (44)

The family and society have complementary functions in defending and fostering the good of each and every human being. (45)

The privatization of religion is a constant danger. This attitude compartmentalizes one's relationship with God, separating it from economic, socio-political, cultural issues. Christians must be constantly challenged to assume their proper role in society by fostering and living a public outlook:

A public outlook among Christians asks them to care for the good ordering of people who are not saved and may never be. It means having concern for arts and letters, the quality of life and its cultural dimensions, the institutions of education and the forms of politics—even if there is no direct payoff for the churches.[9]

This linkage to the larger social whole was a major concern at the Second Vatican Council: the Church is to participate in the amelioration of the world by being socially conscious and politically concerned. Again this vision is shared in *Familiaris Consortio*. Families are to participate in social happenings in dynamic and varied ways. Non-involvement will often threaten human dignity and justice since a vacuum will be created if people abdicate their duty of articulating and living Christian values.

The notion of responsibility underlies the mutual relationship between family and society. This responsibility is grounded in power. The individual, the family, the society, the Church and the State, all possess this ability to bring about or prevent change. When all these parties exercise responsible power in fostering the common good, then justice and peace result. The common good is served. Yet vested interest tends to direct energies and gifts meant for the growth of the community toward self-serving and self-preserving needs and wants. Injustice is effected and society and the family are greatly harmed. The exercise of power for the common good and the proper assumption of responsibility by each grouping are of vital importance to the Church and the modern world.

Rugged individualism will continue to thwart the creation of a healthy society. Narrow parochialism, social myopia, crass apathy, indulgent consumerism, arrogant nationalism are cancer sores that mar and rend the human heart and human family. Society will never be rid of these illnesses but they can be minimized by fostering a social consciousness that truly sees others as one's brothers and sisters. This consciousness begins at home or it never begins at all. Parents enrich society by their involvement in societal and political issues and by encouraging their children to participate as fully as they can.

THEME 8: CHURCH
THESIS: *The family as the domestic Church gets its true identity and sense of purpose from its ecclesial nature.*

Christian marriage and the Christian family build up the Church: for in the family the human person is not only brought into being and progressively introduced by means of education into the human community, but by means of the rebirth of baptism and education in the faith the child is also introduced into God's family, which is the Church. (15)

Among the fundamental tasks of the Christian family is its ecclesial task: the family is placed at the service of the building up of the Kingdom of God in history by participating in the life and mission of the Church. (49)

The Church, a prophetic, priestly and kingly people, is endowed with the mission of bringing all human beings to accept the word of God in faith, to celebrate and profess it in the sacraments and in prayer, and to give expression to it in the concrete realities of life in accordance with the gift and new commandment of love. (63)

There is a rich symbiotic relationship between the family and the Church. They need each other; they enrich each other. Through the family new life is raised up, potential members of God's family; through the Church, the grace of baptism gives entrance into the community of disciples. The family is as integral to the Church as cells are to the body. Both the community of the family and the Church are about the same task: acceptance and proclamation of the Good News, worship in spirit and in truth, service to those in need out of love, the building up of the Kingdom. In a special way the Church does this through sacramental, apostolic and educational avenues; the family does it by living faith, hope and love in ordinary and concrete situations.

Several times in this apostolic exhortation Pope John Paul II stresses the building of the Kingdom of God in history. Our liturgy describes some aspects of that Kingdom:

a kingdom of truth and life,
a kingdom of holiness and grace,
a kingdom of justice, love and peace.[10]

The Church and family intersect at this junction. Both strive to promote the realities of God's saving mysteries. Both are at the service of Jesus, the Lord of heaven and earth. Both find in him truth and life; in him oneness with the Father; in him the love that makes justice and peace a reality. Christ Jesus is the center of the Christian home and the Church. Romano Guardini refreshes our faltering memories:

> "Faith" in the sense of the New Testament means not only religious trust, reverence, self-surrender, but something specific: man's relationship to Christ and to the God who speaks through him which Christ demanded.[11]

Two phenomena characterize the twentieth century: confusion about identity and the subsequent loss of meaning. Who are we? What are we to do? What is our destiny? The Church has a self-understanding that embraces mystery. Yet the task is clear: be a prophetic, kingly and priestly people! With such a vision the Christian family comes to its own self-understanding: the family also is to be a community of persons and the task and mission is the same as the Church's. No small grace here. Amid all the confusion and ambiguity a sense of direction and purpose emerges. Energies can now be directed in meaningful ways. The Christian family is deeply enriched by seeing and living this relationship with the Church.

THEME 9: VALUES
THESIS: *Family life is grounded in the knowledge and expression of basic Gospel values.*

Christian families can do this [bear witness to the Kingdom and the peace of Christ] through their educational activity—that is to say by presenting to their children a model of life based on the values of truth, freedom, justice and love—both through active and responsible involvement in the authentically human growth of society and its institutions, and by supporting in various ways the associations specifically devoted to international issues. (48)

The Christian family also builds up the Kingdom of God in history through the everyday realities that concern and distinguish its state of life. It is thus in the love between husband and wife and between the members of the family—a love lived out in all its extraordinary richness of values and demands: totality, oneness, fidelity and fruitfulness—that the Christian family's participation in the prophetic, priestly and kingly mission of Jesus Christ and of his Church finds expression and realization. (50)

Many negative phenomena which are today noted with regret in family life derive from the fact that, in the new situations, young people not only lose sight of the correct hierarchy of values but, since they no longer have certain criteria of behavior, they do not know how to face and deal with the new difficulties. (66)

Freedom, truth, justice, love, totality, oneness, fidelity, fruitfulness! These are the pillars (values) that support the community of persons we call the family, society and Church. The importance of these values can readily be seen in contrast to their opposites: enslavement, falsity, injustice, hatred, non-commitment, division, infidelity, sterility. None of these categories are ultimately abstract; they are not esoteric philosophical constructs. Rather, they provide the attitudinal base from which life is lived. Values shape decisions which in turn terminate in concrete action. Our actions have consequences that either humanize or destroy people.

In evaluating our lives we move beyond specific, individual acts to the root system—the values from whence they flow. These values truly characterize the essence of our personality. Choices in life! To teach in the catechetical program or spend more time with the children; to build a new room onto the house or give more money to the poor; to take in a refugee child or prod the government to promote international justice. These choices are not necessarily exclusive but a theology of limitation restricts how much we can do. The formation of conscience is based not only on values but also the ordering of these values. What is helpful here is a guiding vision:

> To be an effective member of the Church . . . one needs a guiding vision. Such a vision should serve to interpret one's experience of life with fellow-believers, to suggest priorities and values, and to indicate ways in which the Church might make itself more effectively present in today's world.[12]

Value-free homes and societies are dissipated homes and societies, lacking direction and purpose. Values provide a sense of meaning.

The constant process of value clarification is urgently needed. The social sciences have methods to discern when values are truly authentic and when they are merely nominal. Internalized values have the markings of free choice, strong affective force and patterned activity. Clarifying our values helps to promote civil discourse, a discourse that is essential to keep our planet partially civilized. When values are confused and misunderstood, debate turns into a diatribe. Political, social and religious issues become muddied and constructive communication ceases. Value clarification is not *the* solution to world problems, but without some clarity there can be no progress. What is true of the larger society is also true of the home. Clear values nourish healthy family life.

THEME 10: DANGERS AND DIFFICULTIES
THESIS: *Inner and outer forces present major challenges to the delicate health of family life.*

On the other hand, however, signs are not lacking of a disturbing degradation of some fundamental values: a mistaken theoretical and practical concept of the independence of the spouses in relation to each other; serious misconceptions regarding the relationship of authority between parents and children; the concrete difficulties that the family itself experiences in the transmission of values; the growing number of divorces; the scourge of abortion; the ever more frequent recourse of sterilization; the appearance of a truly contraceptive mentality. (6)

Consequently, faced with a society that is running the risk of becoming more and more depersonalized and standardized and therefore inhuman and dehumanizing, with the negative results of many forms of escapism—such as alcoholism, drugs and even terrorism—the family possesses and continues still to release formidable energies capable of taking man out of his anonymity, keeping him conscious of his personal dignity, enriching him with deep humanity and actively placing him, in his uniqueness and unrepeatability, within the fabric of society. (43)

Among the more troubling signs of this phenomenon [obscuring of certain fundamental values], the Synod Fathers stressed the following, in particular: the spread of divorce and of recourse to a new union, even on the part of the faithful; the acceptance of purely civil marriage in contradiction to the vocation of the baptized to "be married in the Lord"; the celebration of the marriage sacrament without living faith, but for other motives; the rejection of the moral norms that guide and promote the human and Christian exercise of sexuality in marriage. (7)

Teilhard de Chardin's work *The Divine Milieu* shows the deepest reverence for the environment, human-divine-natural, that surrounds and sustains us. When that environment is affected adversely, there is a breakdown in the rich interdependence of all life. Family life is no exception to this universal phenomenon. Certain negative attitudes are in the air and certain ways of relating are becoming accepted that are injurious and destructive of communities of persons; divorce that rends and tears the hearts and minds of parents and children; misunderstanding and subsequent misuse of the gift and beauty of sexuality; erroneous attitudes regarding freedom; a striving for a type of independence that makes relationships impossible. The litany is long and off-key; the pain and the hurt are even more far reaching and dissonant.

Realism demands that we share the full portrait. Healthy family life does survive and is the source of much hope and joy. There are homes where children rejoice in the love and care shown by their parents; there are homes in which youth are given a sense of dignity and respect; there are homes that are sites of caring education and gracious growth. God has promised his presence to the family and with that presence comes the grace to fulfill that unique and noble vocation of every home—the sharing of love.

Familiaris Consortio offers a blueprint charting the waterways of family life. The journey of Lewis and Clark was filled with many unnecessary delays and detours because of the lack of maps. Though they do not remove the struggle of the journey, maps do help in marking the way. The papal exhortation continues the apostolic mission: revealing the mystery of God's love and forgiveness which makes possible community and the building of the Kingdom in which we hear and respond with love to the voice of the Lord.

160 THEMES AND THESES

Footnotes

1. Parker J. Palmer, *The Company of Strangers* (New York: Crossroad, 1981), 33.
2. Anwar el-Sadat, *In Search of Identity* (New York: Harper & Row, 1977), 82.
3. Barbara Tuchman, *A Distant Mirror* (New York: Alfred A. Knopf, Inc., 1978), 97.
4. William Luce, *The Belle of Amherst* (Boston: Houghton Mifflin Company, 1976), 30.
5. Fyodor Dostoevsky, *The Brothers Karamazov* (New York: International Collectors Library, 1941), 171.
6. Romano Guardini, *The Lord* (Chicago: Henry Regnery Company, 1954), 94.
7. Jon Sobrino, S.J., *Christology at the Crossroads*, trans. by John Drury (New York: Orbis Books, 1978), 281.
8. E. Herman, *Creative Prayer* (Cincinnati, Ohio: Forward Movement Publications), 33.
9. Reflection of Martin E. Marty in the foreword to Parker J. Palmer's *The Company of Strangers*, 13.
10. Preface for the Feast of Christ the King.
11. Romano Guardini, 436.
12. Avery Dulles, "Imaging the Church for the 1980's," *Thought*, vol. 56, no. 221 (June, 1981), 121.

**Additional publications and cassettes
by Bishop Robert F. Morneau**

SPIRITUAL AIDS FOR THOSE IN
RENEW:
Ponderings, Poems and Promises

Bishop Morneau reflects in a delightful way on all the aspects of
the *RENEW* program and its tremendous potential for bringing
about a wholistic vitalization of people, parishes and diocese. The
preacher and teacher will find here innumerable insights applic-
able to a variety of speaking situations. The book is further en-
hanced by poignant poems by Bishop Morneau himself and also
Barbara J. Holt and Brother Edward Siefert, F.S.C. **$4.50, paper**

TABLE OF CONTENTS

Preface
God's Call
One Valentine Day
Humpty Dumpty's Dilemma
The Domestic Church
Lest The Parish Perish
He Ain't Heavy
Characterless Caterpillar
Our Response
Look Before You Leap
Moral Cancer
Raised Eyebrows
Fill In The Blank
Where Do You Live?
Learn A Lesson From The Redwood
Empowerment Of The Spirit
You Do What?
The Power And The Glory
Mission Impossible

Spitballers Beware
One Of These Days
No Utopian Camelot
Discipleship
R.S.V.P.
The Lone Ranger Is Dead
A Vitamin A Day Keeps . . .
How Much Does It Cost?
Scars Revisited
Taking The Stand
Evangelization
The Infection Of Faith
Will It Fly?
Once Upon A Time
There's Room In The Inn
Star-Gazing
The Party's Over—Or Is It?
Discussion Questions

SPIRITUALITY AND SOCIAL JUSTICE
Bishop Robert Morneau

". . . this program will help bring clarity and understanding to the call of justice and peace as it comes from the Gospels, and from such documents as *Mater et Magistra, Pacem in Terris* and other more recent church documents." *Religion Teacher's Journal*

TAH130—7 cassettes in dustproof shelf-case—**$53.95**

SPIRITUALITY AND HUMAN GROWTH
Bishop Robert Morneau

An eight-cassette program recorded at a three-week workshop at St. Norbert College brings a remarkable blending of deep spirituality, fine literary awareness and sensitivity and a theological-historical awareness of 14 subjects.

TAH097—14 talks on 8 cassettes with outlines—**$59.95**
Each cassettes is available separately at **$7.95**

TAH097A—**Loneliness/Growth**
TAH097B—**Person/Meaning**
TAH097C—**Courage/Longing**
TAH097D—**Suffering/Death**
TAH097E—**Creativity**
TAH097F—**Intimacy**
TAH097G—**Weakness/Time**
TAH097H—**Joy/Contemplation**

These titles are available at your local **BOOKSTORE** or from:

Alba House Publications
Society of St. Paul
2187 Victory Blvd.
Staten Island, N.Y. 10314-6603